A Locket Of Love

Naomi Sharp

ISBN- 10: 1539863794
ISBN-13 :978- 1539863793

DEDICATION

I dedicate this book to Karen and Jon for the incredible experience of oneness with others, nature and life.

CONTENTS

1 OFF TO SEE NANA O

As Molly let her head rest against the back of the car seat, her mum in front of her was humming along to a song on the radio. Molly turned her head and watched the world pass by in a blur as they drove along, weaving around the country roads. All the autumn colours flickered red, orange and brown as the leaves floated from the branches to the ground heralding the approaching winter months.

'Mum', Molly asked, 'Yes, love?', 'Are we nearly there yet?' Molly grumbled. Her mum looked in the rear view mirror at Molly sitting limp on the back seat 'Not far now, love'. Molly let out a deep sigh – she knew her mum's "not fars" meant that it could be 5 minutes, 50 minutes or even 5 hours away. Molly continued to look out of the window at the hills covered in trees. 'I wish Nana O didn't live so far away' Molly muttered to herself.

Suddenly the car screeched to a halt as Molly's mum slammed on the brakes. Molly was catapulted forward but her seat belt caught her and flung her back into the seat. Molly's mum was already saying harsh words as a pheasant casually meandered out into the road, deciding whether to go forward or turn and head back the way it came.

Molly's mum continued shouting at the pheasant, which was still standing in the middle of the road, as she reached the crescendo in her verbal abuse of the bird. The car horn drowned out the remaining words she spoke and the pheasant flew off. Molly became a statue in her seat, holding her breath. She didn't want to draw any attention to herself in case she ended up being on the receiving end of her mum's temper.

Molly watched the pheasant fly off. 'Lucky thing', she thought. The car jerked into motion as Molly's mum sped off. As they drove further on, gears grinding into place, it was no longer a pleasant journey. The car swerved sharply left and right around the corners as Molly's mum's anger continued to grow. Molly took hold of the car door hand rail in an attempt to avoid being swung around in the back of the car.

There was one more sharp swerve to the left and then the car came to an abrupt halt. Molly let out a sigh and took a deep breath in, filling her body back up with oxygen which made her feel light headed.

She reached down and pressed the button on her seat belt. It pinged back and was poised ready to carry out its next duty of protecting another passenger, like a bodyguard. Molly could hear her mum grunting to herself 'I'll be glad when I don't have to do this journey any more, flipping pheasant thinking he owns the road'. Molly's mum turned around in her seat to face Molly, 'Now remember, your Nana O is getting old so don't cause her any trouble' she said through gritted teeth.

Molly just nodded and reached for the car door handle, opening the door and jumping out. As she closed the door Molly looked at the little cottage, set in the hills with roses climbing up the side of the cottage walls. The house looked tired and in need of some fixing up but there was something about this cottage that Molly loved, it always felt magical, mysterious, like the walls were going to start speaking at any moment, sharing stories of all the things they had seen and heard.

Molly smiled and made her way round to the back of the car where her mum had already started to lift out the bags of shopping. She took hold of one of the bags and made her way up the garden path. Her mum followed behind her with the rest of the shopping. Molly turned the handle of the front door and instead of the door creaking open, it glided, just as if someone was helping to open it from the other side.

Molly looked behind the door but no one was there. Molly paused on the door step. Molly's mum pushed past her and was already in the kitchen and starting to unpack the shopping when Molly stepped into the cottage.

Molly suddenly jumped back, dropping her bag, 'Argh!' she screamed, clutching her chest. She heard a chuckle as she began to compose herself. 'What's wrong with you? You look like you have just seen a ghost', Nana O chuckled in her husky voice from the kitchen doorway. 'Nana O you made me jump!' Molly said as she picked up the shopping bag.

'So I see' Nana O said as she made her way back into the kitchen where Molly's mum was still unpacking the shopping. Molly followed her in and placed the bag she was carrying onto the kitchen worktop. Nana O filled the kettle with water and brought the teapot to the front of the worktop, placing fresh tea leaves in the strainer. Molly was already in the biscuit cupboard getting out the biscuit barrel and placing it on the table.

Having tea at Nana O's was like having tea with the queen. Nana O got out the best china cups and saucers along with a bowl of sugar cubes and jug of milk. She placed a plate in front of Molly, 'Be a darling and put a few biscuits on there for us' Nana O said, gesturing to the plate.

Molly could never understand why the biscuits needed to go on a plate first when they were all going to end up in the same place: her stomach! But Molly did as she was asked and piled the biscuits onto the plate. She watched Nana O shuffle around the kitchen, hunched over. Molly didn't know anyone else as old as her Nana, with her wrinkles carved into her face and her frail body. Her eyes, however, always had a cheeky sparkle to them, like they had seen a lot, been through a lot, and knew the mysteries and secrets of the world and of life.

Molly was brought back from her thoughts as her mum pulled out another chair which made a screeching noise on the tiled floor. Molly's mum sat down at the table and Molly brought the plate across and placed it on the table next to her. Nana O brought across the teapot. She held the tea strainer over each cup to catch any tea leaves that might escape, and placed a cup in front of each of them.

After putting in the milk, Molly's mum then placed one sugar lump in her tea; Molly copied. Molly stared at her mum as she knew her mum was just counting the minutes until they could go, until she had spent a reasonably acceptable time with her mum and she could make her excuses and leave.

Molly looked at her Nana O, who was happy to have the company but knew her daughter's agenda. However, she still enjoyed the moment for what it was even though her daughter's intentions were not benign.

Nana O broke the silence, 'So, Molly, how are your friends Dillon and Layla?' 'Annoying as usual' Molly said in a huff as she thought of her best friends who lived on the next street. Wherever Molly was, Dillon and Layla were never far away. 'Dillon keeps beating me at sports' Molly said with disgust. Nana O smiled as she sipped her tea.

Molly's mum sat silent. Molly reached for another biscuit as more of her tea was being absorbed by biscuits than drank by her. Molly smiled to herself as this was one of the best things about coming round to Nana O's house – the endless supply of biscuits ... and her stories. 'I wonder if we will have time for one of her stories today?', Molly thought.

Nana O reached for the teapot to refill the cups. She reached across to begin filling her daughter's cup. Molly's mum placed her hand over the top of the cup, covering it 'Not for me, thanks, otherwise I will be needing the toilet on the drive home'. Nana O brought back the teapot and filled up her own cup. She didn't respond to the comment and just smiled instead.

'If you will excuse me' Molly's mum said, getting up from the kitchen table, 'I'll just make a start on your washing and ironing'. She made her way out of the kitchen, leaving Molly and Nana O alone. Molly swirled the remaining tea with bits of biscuits floating around in her cup. 'Do you think we will have time for a story Nana O?' she asked shyly.

Nana O took another sip of tea and placed her cup back on her saucer with a chink. 'Of course, darling, but first we need to light the fire and I need to wash the pots. Be a darling and go outside to the shed and bring a basketful of wood back with you' Nana O said peacefully. She made her way over to the kitchen sink and began to wash the empty cups. 'Oh Nana O, I hate that creepy shed, I swear it's going to fall down on me one of these days, not to mention all the slugs and spiders, and there is probably a giant deadly snake in there waiting to get me' Molly pleaded.

Nana O continued to wash the pots in silence. Molly knew what that meant: Nana O wasn't asking, she was telling. Just then they heard her mum stomp down the stairs. As she reached the bottom she stubbed her toe on one of Nana O's many statues that were scattered around the cottage. 'You....' and Molly's mum looked up to see the two of them looking at her.

'Never mind' Molly's mum said through gritted teeth, as she disappeared into the utility room. Molly took the opportunity to leave the room as the shed began to look more appealing in comparison to the wrath of her mum's anger. Molly made her way out of the front door, picking up the basket which was already waiting by the front door to be filled, and headed round to the back of the house to the shed, which was now slightly leaning to the left.

Molly took a deep breath and opened the door. A shiver ran down her back. Molly leant in, making sure her feet stayed outside as she peered around for anything that might land on her or jump out. 'Hello' she said 'If you could all just stay where you are whilst I just fill the basket up and then I'll leave you to whatever you were doing' Molly whispered. She knew the creatures didn't understand English but it made her feel better.

Molly placed the basket just inside the door and started to fill it up as quickly as she could by grabbing as much wood as possible in her small hands. Then she scooped up the basket and ran as fast as she could back to the cottage, flinging the front door open. It made a large bang as it hit the wall; Molly threw the basket into the living room.

Rubbing and flicking her body as if there were millions of ants crawling over her, she finished with a big shake 'Yuk – creepy, grimy shed' she muttered to herself. Nana O picked up the basket and took the wood across to the fireplace.

'Be a darling and fetch yesterday's newspaper from the kitchen and bring it over' Nana O said whilst she began to place the pieces of wood into the open fire. Molly went into the kitchen as silent as a mouse, trying not to be seen by her mum. She grabbed the newspaper and headed back into the living room at a sprint to where it was safe. Her mum was never as cross when Nana O was around.

Molly passed the newspaper across to Nana O who scrunched up the pages and placed them into the fire. With a strike of the match the fire was ablaze and burning bright. Molly was always amazed by Nana O's ability to get a roaring fire going so quickly. Nana O saw Molly's expression of amazement, 'When you have been doing it for as long as I have then you too will be able to get a blazing fire from a single match' Nana O said wisely.

She leant over and reached for the arm of her favourite chair positioned next to the fire and let out a sigh as she lowered herself into it. She shuffled around as she got comfortable, settling in for the rest of the day. On the small table next to the chair was two sets of glasses, a glass of water, today's newspaper, a toffee sweet, an alarm clock and the pills the doctor had given her to take.

Molly fetched a small three legged wooden stool with an acorn carved into the seat. She brought it across and put it in front of where Nana O sat, ready to hear the story. Just as Nana O was about to begin, Molly's mum came in with her arms full of freshly ironed sheets. She looked at what was happening in the living room. 'Don't get too comfy as we'll be going in a few minutes', Molly's mum said. She stared at Molly, clearly not wanting to stay any longer than she had to.

'Of course not, darling, Molly was just telling me what her, Layla and Dillon had been up to' Nana O responded casually. Molly felt her mum's gaze burn deep inside of her; she quickly broke eye contact and stared at the fire.

They watched Molly's mum exit the room and listened as she stomped back up the stairs. Molly just continued to stare at the fire, wishing she could become invisible. Nana O saw Molly sitting there on the stool like a frozen statue but not like any statue that she had around her cottage – her statues always looked happy.

Molly looked frightened but, most of all, sad. Just then Nana O knew exactly what story she would tell today. 'Right, let's begin' Nana O announced, bringing Molly out of her gaze. Molly turned back to face Nana O, 'This story is...'. As Nana O began she was rudely interrupted by the alarm on the table next to her going off.

BEEP BEEP BEEP, 'Blooming thing' Nana O said, firmly pressing a button on the alarm. 'That alarm's going to be the death of me' she grumbled. They then heard Molly's mum's voice pierce down through the air from upstairs, 'Don't forget to take your tablets!'. Nana O picked up the box from the table by the side of the chair and unclipped the compartment that said "today" on the lid. She emptied the different coloured tablets into her hand. She then placed the box back on the table and in one smooth movement she tossed the tablets into the fire and they were quickly swallowed up by the flames.

'All done, darling!', Nana O called up to Molly's mum. Molly sat there shocked, with her mouth wide open. She couldn't believe what she had just witnessed – her Nana O being rebellious! She had never seen this side of her Nana before. Nana O readjusted herself in the chair with the corners of her mouth curling up as she tried her hardest to hide the smile of satisfaction from her act of defiance.

Molly looked at Nana O then at the fire then back at Nana O. Molly shook her head in disbelief. 'I have been doing just fine for the last 90 years with a good lifestyle, a happy mind and heart. I don't need those things flowing around my veins. I'll go when I am ready and no sooner' Nana O proclaimed.

Then Nana O became still, 'Before I begin our story is there anything you want to tell me Molly?' Nana O asked lovingly. Molly shuffled uncomfortably on her stool, avoiding eye contact with Nana O. 'No, everything is fine' Molly said with a shooting pain going through her heart. She hated lying to her Nana so much but the pain of telling her the truth was greater than the pain of lying, or so she thought.

'Very well then', Nana O's gaze held on Molly. She knew full well that deep inside of Molly was a chamber full of secrets, of fears that she was too afraid to let out into the light. Nana O looked at the fire. She had been around long enough to know that things would take their own course, that they would come out in time, when Molly was ready. 'Maybe we could spur things on' Nana O thought as her eyes began to glisten with hope.

Nana O placed her hands on the centre of her lap. The room was filled with a feeling of warmth, the different colours from the objects around the room began to radiate more brightly. Molly got goose bumps as she looked around; her gaze finally reached Nana O whose breathing had slowed, making her look more peaceful and relaxed. Her wrinkles were less defined and her skin glowed as she sat in her chair. Nana watched Molly take in the surroundings and noticed that she had a puzzled look on her face from what she saw. Nana O smiled to herself. 'We will save that story for another day' she thought.

'Are we ready to begin?' Nana O said, bringing Molly back from her thoughts and into the present moment. 'Yes, absolutely' Molly said eagerly, waiting to hear where the story was going to take her. Nana O cleared her throat as if she was about to tell the story to every single person in the world.

2 THE TALE THAT CHANGED THE WORLD

'To begin with, you should know that the story you are about to hear began many years ago, and has been passed from person to person, generation to generation. It continues to bring magic to millions of people's lives, and I am sure it will continue to be told for many years from now', Nana O said, proud to be part of the heritage of this legacy.

Molly was leaning forward with her elbows resting on her knees and her hands cupping her head, barely blinking as she became captivated in what her Nana O had said. 'Does this mean that I am now part of the legacy?' Molly asked, curious of what this meant. 'Well, that is your choice. If you share this story with someone else you have become connected to all those who have been part of this story from the past, present and future'.

Molly sat quietly, not fully understanding how a story could connect so many people. She decided she would save that question for later, as the anticipation and excitement was building inside of her like a volcano that was about to erupt.

Nana O sat quietly for a moment watching Molly become more restless, however, she enjoyed adding some suspense to the story that was about to be told. 'The story begins with a man called Jacob. He was out walking as he did every day with his dog, along a dirt track that wound over the rolling hills. As he casually walked along the path, watching his dog bound up and down the hillside, he let out a sigh as he got a tingle in his stomach. This was his time during the day to just have some peace and quiet from life, from his wife asking him to do jobs, the kids wanting to play and his annoying boss always picking faults with his work. He looked down at his dog that had returned and was now back by his side obediently awaiting his next command.

'Go on, you go and have some fun, one of us might as well' Jacob said to his dog as he continued to trudge along the muddy path. As he walked, only hearing his own footsteps squelch in the mud, he became preoccupied with thinking about the day he had had, as he recalled the argument he had had earlier with his boss. As he became engrossed, reliving the argument again in his mind, he kicked a small rock that was in his way on the path with frustration. As the rock rolled away a piece of mud flew up and went splat on his trousers. 'Just my bloody luck, I have just had these cleaned!' he exclaimed in anger as he tried to wipe off the mud. Instead he smudged and smeared it even more into his clean trousers.

He threw his hands up in the sky 'Why? Why me? Can you not just pick on someone else for the day?!' he said to the clouds that were gently floating through the sky. As Jacob took his next step, he hadn't noticed his dog return and sit in front of him, waiting. Jacob spotted the dog as his leg was in mid air but it was already too late – he quickly took a step to the side, causing him to wobble off balance.

He landed with a thump on his bum in the mud. He lifted his hands to survey the damage and saw dirt and sloppy mud dripping off his fingers. Jacob let out a big sigh, if it had been anyone else it would have been funny, but not for him. This was just one more piece of bad luck to add to his day, week, even life. He looked to his left at his dog who was still sitting in the same spot, with its ears pricked up and head tilted to one side, staring right back at him.

'What are you looking at mutt?' he grunted. The dog barked in response to his words. Jacob began to stand up, covering himself in even more mud in the process. As he came to an upright position something caught his eye. Something that glistened in the mud where the rock had been.

The man took a second glance and reached down, moving a lump of clay out of the way, and there laid a silver locket. He picked it up as the chain intertwined between his fingers. 'Hmm, that's pretty' he said to himself, trying to wipe off the mud that was covering the locket on his already muddy trousers. He looked around to see if anyone else was there. He looked down the hill where you could see the winding path continue to weave its way through the land. No one was there. 'I'll leave it at the gate at the bottom of the path where the car park is in case someone comes back for it' he said to himself as he placed it in his coat pocket and continued to walk.

As he made his way along the footpath his mind wandered back to what waited for him at the bottom of the hill. He let out another sigh as he watched his dog bound around with excitement and joy at the different smells, splashing through the puddles, watching mud fly up and cover his fur. 'I wish I could be more care free like you' he mumbled to himself as the dog came bounding back to him. The dog barked and nudged the man's hand so it became placed on the dog's head, signalling for a stroke.

The man smiled and ruffled the dog's fur, covering him in even more mud. 'Come on you, we'd best be heading back or they will think I have done a runner'. Jacob picked up the pace as they walked the last bit to the car park. As he reached the car he pulled out his keys and the car lights flashed as it unlocked. He lifted the car boot door open and the dog jumped straight in and laid down. The man looked at the different coloured dog that was now in his car, stained with mud, compared to the dog he had begun the walk with.

'I think you'll need a hose down before you are allowed in the house' the man said to the dog. The dog put its paw over his nose in protest; the man chuckled as he closed the boot and made his way round to the driver's side. He shook his head. 'Sometimes I swear you understand what I'm saying' he muttered to himself as he thought about the dog's reaction. Jacob climbed in, smearing mud on the leather seats. He suddenly became surprised as he found himself just smiling instead of his usual reaction of grumbling. 'It'll wipe off' he thought as he began to reverse.

Just as the car was in motion another car came straight behind him, cutting him up. Jacob slammed on the brakes, sending the dog flying into the back seat. He looked in his rear view mirror and was just about to start shouting at the other driver as he felt his usual hatred towards people build, but then he found himself instead waving to the person as they passed him by. 'That's weird' he thought as he realised the way he had just reacted. He shook his head, 'the stress of everything lately must be making me act weird' Jacob said dismissively.

Jacob started to press the accelerator and continued to reverse, turning the car he made his way out of the car park. As he drove along he noticed the lovely spring flowers along the roadside, the trees starting to get their spring leaves. 'I didn't realise how beautiful this road is' he said as he looked in the rear view mirror at his dog in the boot. The dog got up and rested his head on the back seat head rest. The man continued to drive, admiring his surroundings as if it was the first time he had ever seen nature's true colours.

As he reached his house he pulled up onto the driveway and the car became silent as he turned off the ignition. He looked through the windscreen at the house in front of him and what lay waiting for him behind the front door. He got out of the car and headed round to the back. As the car boot door opened the dog jumped out, stopping straight away to have a shake. As his whole body shook, sending pieces of mud flying into the air, Jacob turned his back to avoid getting his face splattered with clay.

He closed the boot door with a slam, slipped the keys into his coat pocket and then made his way to the garden gate where his dog was already waiting. As he made his way through the dog zoomed past him towards the back door. 'Ha wishful thinking' Jacob sung. As he entered the back garden he made his way to where the hose pipe lay, reaching and taking hold of it and turning it on. The dog didn't move from where he stood by the back door, staring at Jacob. 'You created it' Jacob said, clicking his fingers to signal for the dog to come and sit by his side.

The dog slowly made his way over with his head hanging low. When he reached him the man showered him in water, watching as the clear water turned brown with all the mud being washed off. As Jacob reached for the tap and turned it off he surveyed his dog. As he stared, he smiled. The dog looked half the size compared to before as all his fur was stuck to his body. The dog seized his opportunity and just before the man had chance to move out of the way, the dog shook again and his vibrating body sent water droplets flying through the air. 'Argh!' Jacob squealed and then couldn't stop himself erupting into a belly roaring laugh.

The back door was flung open and a young girl appeared. She looked up and down at her dad covered in mud and their dog wet through. The dog saw the opportunity and made a dash for the small gap between the little girl and the open door. 'No, don't let the dog in!' Jacob said but before the words had left his mouth, the dog had disappeared inside.

The dog returned a moment later as his wife brought him back outside by his collar, with a towel in her other hand. She handed Jacob the dog and the towel, not saying a word. She didn't need to, however, as her look spoke a thousand words. Jacob smiled sheepishly, 'Hi love' he said, reaching for the dog and towel. His wife just turned and went back inside, closing the door behind her. He rubbed the dog with the towel 'One day you are going to get us both into so much trouble' he said playfully as the dog disappeared under a towel.

He opened the door and the dog made his way in. Jacob slipped off his wellies and reached into his coat pocket to take out his keys. His hand reached the bottom of the pocket but he didn't feel his keys, instead he felt something else. He lifted it out and there in his hand was the locket. 'Damn' he said with frustration. 'I was meant to leave this back at the gate' he mused as he stared at the locket, glistening in the light. He laid the locket in the palm of his hand and as he turned it over he noticed there was a star engraved on it.

'Maybe there's a picture inside of who it belongs to to give me a clue'. He began to recall the different people he saw regularly walking their dogs along the same path. He made his way into the kitchen and fetched the cloth resting by the sink. He started to wipe the locket and the locket began to transform from dull to shiny and gleaming. Jacob took hold of the clasp and the locket made a "click" sound as it opened up. Jacob stopped and stared at what he saw;

there were no pictures but instead there was a small strip of paper. He gently took the piece of paper out and lifted it up.

Molly's mum appeared at the doorway to the living room, surprising Molly and Nana O out of their story and back into reality. 'Another 10 minutes and then we have to go' Molly's mum said with relief in her voice. Molly was just about to protest but before she could her mum interjected '10 minutes', this time saying it more sternly. 'Yes, mum' Molly replied feeling gutted.

She turned back to Nana O. 'What did the piece of paper say?' she said eagerly. 'Maybe we should leave that for the next time I see you' Nana O said, knowing full well the reaction she was going to get off Molly. 'No!' Molly exclaimed. 'I won't be able to last that long' she continued. Nana O began to chuckle as she saw the sparkle of excitement return to Molly's eyes, as she once again got lost in a land of dreams which took her away from her present troubles.

'Very well, where was I?' Nana O said, staring back into the fire. 'Jacob had just opened the locket and lifted out a piece of paper with some writing on it' Molly said impatiently. 'Ah, yes, I remember'.

'Just as he began to focus on the words written on the piece of paper his wife came rushing into the kitchen like a whirlwind. She suddenly stopped and looked over at her husband who was standing looking confused, still in his outside jacket covered in mud. 'What's that?' she asked. He quickly closed the locket and stuffed it back into his coat pocket. 'Nothing. Just something I found on the walk. I'm going to leave it on the gate tomorrow. I meant to leave it today but I got sidetracked'. His wife gave him the once over. Even though she didn't believe his story she had more important things to be getting on with' Nana O continued.

'No, Nana O, that's not how it goes. He reads the note and then his wife enters' Molly said with a cheeky grin, desperate to know what was written on the piece of paper inside the locket. 'Is that so? And who is the story teller?' Nana O said, trying to conceal her smile.

'Shall I continue?' Nana O added. 'Yes please' Molly said quickly, not wanting any more delays. 'Jacob made his way back into the utility room and took off his coat, hanging it above his wellies. He looked behind him, no one was there. He put his hand back in his coat pocket and took out the locket, opened it up, and took hold of the piece of paper again. He lifted it to the light and read 'Love is your answer, wishes come true as you remember the place that connects me and you'. 'What?' the man said, surprised he repeated it aloud and looking out of the window to try to make sense of the words. With a puzzled look he quickly put the piece of paper back in the locket and placed it in his coat pocket. Spinning round he headed back into the kitchen to be greeted by his family who had already begun to gather around the table for dinner.

'Ah, that's disappointing' Molly said as she sat up and readjusted herself on the stool she was sitting on. 'Saying wishes come true is a lie. It's something you tell kids to distract them. And the answer is bogus – he didn't even ask a question!' Molly said proudly, pretending to act grown up. Nana O raised her eyebrows, looking surprised at what she had just witnessed.

'Well, I don't know who's been telling you that rubbish but wishes do come true, and it's love that brings the wishes to life and there is something inside of us all that helps connects us, taking us to the place where we can receive the wish we have made' Nana O said placing her hands on the arms of the chair. Molly moved uncomfortably on her stool at Nana O's response. She thought that wishes coming true was just hearsay. Nana O watched as the confusion settled over Molly's mind. 'Any wish you make will come true if you believe it will come true and he did ask a question whilst he was walking' Nana O began to explain. 'Well' Molly said interrupting her and standing up from her stool 'I have made a whole bunch of wishes and none of them have ever come true, you're wrong Nana O' she said, trying to hide the distress in her voice which wobbled as the words left her mouth.

'Just you sit back down on that stool and listen to your Nana O, that's enough of you talking absolute twaddle'. Nana O leant forward in her chair, getting closer to Molly who had just sat back down folding her arms across her chest in protest. Nana O wanted to make sure that Molly could clearly hear each and every word she was about to speak. 'Do you know what Hope is?' Nana O asked, staring deep into Molly's eyes. 'Of course I do, doesn't everyone?' Molly said, tightening her arms. 'Obviously not' Nana O said, lifting her eyebrows again at Molly's response. Molly shifted her gaze as she felt the power of Nana O. Sometimes it felt like Nana O could read her thoughts.

'Hope is to wish for and welcome something, with the expectation of its fulfilment with confidence and belief that it will come true. It is to desire something with little reason or justification' Nana O paused 'so all wishes will come true if you believe with all your heart they are going to come true'.

Molly's arms began to relax as she thought about what she had just heard. Nana O sat back in her chair watching the tornado of thoughts going around Molly's mind. 'But ... that ...it can't ...' Molly couldn't find the words. Molly let out a big sigh, letting her arms flop to her side. She looked at Nana O shaking her head, not even knowing why. Nana O's head lifted back as a roar of laughter flung out of her body echoing around the room.

'It's not funny Nana O' Molly said trying not to comply with her urge of joining in the laughter too. Nana O tried to respond but couldn't fit the words in between her laughs. Molly sat there watching her Nana O in hysterics, she sat waiting and waiting some more. Eventually Nana O began to calm down, with a laugh now and then escaping into the air. 'So are you going to tell me what was so funny?' Molly said sternly, not amused at all by her Nana O's antics.

Nana O readjusted her position in the chair, wiping the tears from the side of her cheeks from the laughter. 'Well they say people are more educated today but all I see is they are being well educated in the twaddle' Nana O said as she began to giggle again. Molly looked at her not knowing what her Nana O was talking about. Molly started to become frustrated with her Nana O and said 'Can we just get back to the story because I have to go soon?' Molly wasn't enjoying the feeling of confusion flowing around her body and she looked back at the door where she was expecting her mum to be standing.

Nana O coughed, clearing her throat again 'Yes, of course. As he sat at the table he listened to his wife trying to negotiate with the children to eat their dinner, as they fidgeted around. Jacob kept quiet watching the chaos whirl around him, then he felt a foot kick his knee. He looked across at his daughter who had suddenly became engrossed with the dinner on her plate whilst trying to hide her smirking.

He lent down, rubbing his knee 'Could you just help for one minute instead of disappearing into your thoughts?' his wife interrupted him. He snapped out of his day dream and stared blankly at her. 'Sorry, what did you say? I was...'. 'I know – thinking' his wife finished his sentence for him.

She screeched the chair back, grabbing the plates and heading towards the sink. The children saw their cue and leapt into action back to their toys. 'Maybe you could help by doing bath time?' his wife said, not looking back as she stared out of the kitchen window. She was trying not to let tonight turn out like every other night – a raging fight saying words of hate they both didn't mean. Jacob continued to stare at her for a moment and thought that this was not the time to disagree with her.

He slowly pushed back his chair, stood up and made his way into the play room where he began the obstacle course of trying to reach the children without injuring himself on toys. He took a step on one small free space of carpet that wasn't occupied by a toy. As he was just about to take the next step, a remote control car came whooshing by his foot causing him to lose his balance. He suddenly grabbed hold of the door frame before he fell over.

'Right you guys you have 60 seconds to get upstairs and undressed ready for your bath!' Jacob bellowed. The kids froze and stared at their dad, they quietly put down their toys and took each other's hands as they made their way out of the play room and up the stairs. As they disappeared out of sight Jacob turned and started to knock his head against the door frame.

As the shame and guilt began to poison his body 'Why am I so stupid?' he said to himself. He immediately regretted what he had just said. He knew his time was precious with his children and instead of joining them having fun he killed the joy all around.

He pushed off from the door frame and began to make his way across to the stairs. As his foot hit the first step of the stairs he heard the children upstairs mumble 'Quick, he's coming' and tiny footsteps pitter patter across the landing. He took hold of the banister and pulled himself up whilst his head hung low as he felt all life leave his body.

As he neared the top he looked up to see the two of them stood there with towels in one hand and pj's in the other, ready for inspection like they were on parade. He paused as he could find no words to restore the life and love in the room that was now lost. Even sorry wasn't the right place to start, finally concluding in his thoughts that just staying quiet was the best option. He managed to give a weak smile as he passed them and went into the bathroom to start to run the bath.

As he watched the bath fill with water he turned to the two of them who had followed him in 'Do you want some bubbles?' 'Yes please daddy' the little girl replied as she glanced across to her brother who gave her a reassuring wink. In that moment the man died a thousand deaths as he saw the effect that his words downstairs had caused. He saw such fear in innocent eyes.

As he added the bubbles he swirled the water round watching the bubbles grow, wishing there was a way to make amends for his actions. The children carefully put their toes in the water, testing the temperature but also testing their dad to see if it was ok to get in. They slithered past him and sank deep into the bath water, enjoying the warmth of the water wrapping around their bodies. The brother took hold of the soap and started to make it froth and wash his sister. Just then a single tear escaped Jacob's eye as he watched the compassion and love between his two children.

He turned to look out of the window and caught the tear with his finger before it began to cascade down his cheek. As he sat he got a strange feeling in his stomach as his gaze fell on his wife's make up bag on the windowsill. Then a smile swept across his face. He knew exactly what they were going to do – they were going to paint the room with fun! Jacob reached for the make up bag and emptied the contents onto the windowsill. Ruffling through the contents for something to write with, the mascara hit the floor. A little hand reached and picked it up, putting it on the edge of the bath. 'Ah! There it is!' he announced with excitement.

The two children looked at each other with confusion and then back at their dad. Before they could ask what it was he was looking for they saw two socks fly across the room, their dad swivel on the edge of the bath and dunk his feet into the bath tub. Rolling up his trouser legs he sent a small tidal wave towards the children. 'Dad!!!' they screamed as it splashed their faces with bubbles causing them to giggle. They watched their dad bring a lipstick from behind his back and took the lid off with a pop.

He leant forward and wrote "d a d" with a letter in each tile on the bathroom wall. 'You are going to be in so much trouble' the girl said excitedly as she repositioned herself to get a better view. Their dad leant forward writing "t r o u b l e" next to it. The boy piped up – add the word 'tractor', and 'pony' the girl shouted, joining in. Then they all began to shout words – 'poo' the boy said, 'unicorn' the girl added, 'family' the dad continued.

He stood up in the bath so he could reach new tiles.

The lipstick became smaller as he wrote and they all watched words fill the bathroom. Just as he was writing the next word "L o..." his wife appeared at the bathroom door as she became curious what they were all laughing about upstairs.

She surveyed the wall with her lipstick all over it, they all froze and then two arms shot up pointing at their dad who was poised with lipstick in hand. He watched as her face transformed from shock to thunder. As she felt the words about to erupt out of her mouth she turned around and went into the bedroom as she knew what she was about to say wasn't for children's ears.

Jacob suddenly turned to his two children in the bath and in a cheeky voice answered back 'Snitches, snitches'. 'You're in trouble, you're in trouble' they replied. Suddenly they heard their mum shout from the bedroom 'bed time!' They all sprung into action as the children leapt out of the bath grabbing their towels, spilling even more water onto the bathroom floor.

They quickly towelled themselves dry and slipped on their pj's, finishing by running into their bedrooms, diving on their beds and snuggling under their duvets. Jacob stepped out of the bath as he placed the lid back on the lipstick and put the make up back in the bag. He walked into their rooms leaving water footprints on the carpet and with his trousers still rolled up he leant over giving them each a kiss 'Night you two'. 'Night, dad' they said in unison. 'Love you dad' a little voice whispered as he pulled the door closed.

He made his way back into the bathroom. He looked at the wall and couldn't help but chuckle to himself. He suddenly felt something being thrusted into his stomach and looked to his left to see his wife with a bottle of cleaner and a cloth. He reached up and took hold of the bottle. 'You made the mess, you clean it up' she said sternly. He leant across kissing her head 'with pleasure' he said, stepping back into the bath and spraying the wall with cleaner.

He listened to his wife's footsteps as they went down the stairs. He started to hum whilst he cleaned the tiles, smiling as he read the words and felt a happy tingle of happiness inside. As he was just finishing wiping the wall, he made a mental note 'Next time don't choose a bright red lipstick, use a lighter shade of pink' as he scrubbed at the last letter.

Jacob reached across and pulled the plug, watching the water disappear down the plughole in a swirl. As he stepped out of the bath he reached to pull the cord for the light and darkness descended on the bathroom. Jacob made his way down the stairs but now there was a spring in his step and he continued to hum a tune that rang in his heart. He walked into the kitchen taking hold of his wife and swinging her around as they began to dance around the kitchen floor.

She was taken aback as she twirled around the room, still holding the orange for the children's packed lunch in her hand. He finished his tune, sealing it with a kiss and turned away to go and sit at the kitchen table. Jacob's wife went back to making the packed lunches as she ran through all the jobs still left to do this evening ready for tomorrow.

Jacob sat at the table still humming his tune and the words continued to play like a broken record in his head. 'Love is the answer, wishes come true as you remember the place that connects me and you'. 'Right! Time to go!' a voice said behind them, making Molly and Nana O jump. They turned round to see Molly's mum stood in the doorway with her coat on. 'Now!' she said as she saw neither Molly nor Nana O make any movement.

'Perfect timing' Nana O said, sliding forward to the front of her chair and beginning to rock forwards and backwards, holding onto the chair arms to gather momentum in order to stand up. With one final push she pushed off from the chair arms to a standing position, taking a moment to find her balance.

Molly stood up and took the stool back to where she got it from, then made her way across the living room to where her mum was standing. She turned to watch

Nana O shuffle across the living room, taking hold of pieces of furniture for balance as she went. Nana O looked so young and full of life when she was telling her story, now she just looks old Molly thought. 'Not old, just wiser' Nana O said as she reached them both.

Molly shuffled uncomfortably where she stood. 'I'm sure I didn't say that out loud she thought to herself'. 'You didn't' Nana O said as she passed them, making her way to the front door. Molly's jaw dropped in disbelief – now things had got super weird.

Molly's mum took no notice of the conversation as she followed Nana O to the door. Molly's mum opened the front door and stepped out into the fresh air. She turned and faced Nana O 'I'll see you in a couple of days' she said, waving as she made her way briskly to the car.

Molly stood in front of Nana O, still trying to figure out how she had known what she was thinking. Nana O stared at Molly, admiring such a bundle of love. How grateful she felt for having the chance to spend time with her. 'Will I be seeing you in a couple of days or will it be another year again?' 'Will you tell me the rest of your story?' Molly asked. She normally hated coming to see her grandma but for some reason she had started to see her differently, a new side of her she had never seen before Molly thought.

'That's because you weren't ready to receive the information' Nana O responded. 'And, yes, you have my word – I will tell the rest of the story'. 'How do you do that?!' Molly exclaimed, throwing her hands up to her head in disbelief. Nana O began to chuckle again 'You'll soon know'.

Molly turned and began to walk down the path. After she had taken a couple of steps she stopped, turning round to look back at Nana O standing in the doorway of her cottage. Molly ran back to Nana O, flinging her arms around her waist, not saying anything but sharing so much.

Then she turned and took off back down the garden path to where her mum was waiting in the car. Molly reached for the car door. As she took hold of the handle she received a static shock, her hand flew off the handle and she shook it in the air. 'That's not happened before' Molly said as she tentatively took hold of the car door handle again. This time there was nothing. She opened the door and slid onto the back seat.

As she pulled the door closed she heard her mum say impatiently 'any time today'. Molly quickly pulled the door shut and put on her seat belt as the car started to move forward and they began to drive back down the lane. They drove past a tree that had grown on the side of the road and there on the lower branches sat an owl. 'That's odd' Molly thought. 'Mum, do you only see owls at night?' Molly asked, turning in her seat to stare at the tree that was getting progressively further away, 'Yes, normally, why?' she asked. 'No reason' Molly replied. Molly watched the cottage getting smaller and smaller out of the back window of the car. When Molly could no longer see the cottage she turned round in her seat to face the front. They drove back home with the radio being the only sound in the car.

3 FROM ONE REALITY TO THE NEXT

As Molly's mum pulled into the driveway of the house, before the car had even come to a halt, Molly's car door was open as she was quickly trying to unclip her seat belt. Molly jumped out of the car as it came to a stop and ran through the front door, up the stairs and into her bedroom.

After a few moments, Molly's mum made her way through the front door and closed it behind her. She headed along the hallway to the kitchen, where she found Molly's dad finishing making the dinner.

'How was your day?' he asked as he made his way over to the kitchen table, placing the knives and forks in front of the three chairs. 'Same old. I wish she wasn't so stubborn and would just get someone in to help her full time. Oh and the best bit is she has been filling Molly's head with her wacky stories again' Molly's mum said as she filled the kettle to make a cup of tea.

Molly's dad made his way back to the cooker where

he started to dish out the dinner, 'That bad, hey?' he said as he took the first plate to the table. 'Yes, and the worst of it is I think Molly believes her' Molly's mum said as stood waiting for the kettle to boil. 'I'm sure it's not that big of a deal – it will be like everything else – she will stop believing in those silly stories the older she gets' he said, placing his hand on her shoulder as he passed her.

'I hope so' Molly's mum said as she finished making her tea and went to sit down at the table, staring into her cup of tea, lost in thought. Molly's dad brought the last two plates across and placed them on the table before heading down the hallway. 'Molly! Dinner's ready' he shouted from the bottom of the stairs before making his way back into the kitchen and sitting at the table. They heard Molly bound down the stairs, her footsteps making a jolly beat as she appeared at the kitchen doorway and joined her parents at the table, her chair screeching on the floor as she dragged it out to sit on it.

'How was your day?' Molly's mum asked Molly's dad, as Molly quietly ate in the background. Something wasn't right she thought, something didn't feel right. Molly decided to eat her dinner as quickly as possible and get back to her bedroom without drawing attention to herself.

'It was good' Molly's dad replied. 'They have asked me if I want to move to another part of the company' he said as he filled his mouth full of food. 'Oh right. Is there any talk of a pay rise?' Molly's mum asked him as she poked the food around on her plate with her fork. 'Not yet but I think the move will give me the opportunity' he said looking at her. Suddenly Molly's mum's fork dropped to the plate. As it hit the plate the noise rang in Molly's ears. 'Thank you for dinner, dad' Molly said, getting up quickly from the table. 'You haven't finished your dinner' he said. 'Not hungry' Molly said, dashing to the stairs and running up to her bedroom, trying to escape the wrath of the storm that was building in the house.

Just as Molly reached her bedroom and was closing the door, she heard her mum from downstairs begin yelling 'You said this was only going to be temporary!' Molly's mum screamed. 'We can't keep living like this' she shouted as Molly heard her mum slam the plate into the sink.

Molly made her way across her bedroom to the windowsill. It had just started to get dark. As the sun was setting the stars began to emerge in the sky. Molly took the blanket that was lying on the floor and pulled herself up on the windowsill. She wrapped herself in the blanket and closed the curtains in the hope that she would turn invisible.

As she sat in her cocoon she continued to watch the night sky grow darker and darker as the sun completely disappeared behind a row of houses.

Staring at the stars, making different pictures and patterns from them, she wished she could be amongst them, away from all the anger that filled the house. Her gaze fell on one star in particular. It wasn't necessarily the brightest but Molly thought it was the most beautiful star out of all of them.

As she let out a large sigh, she remembered Nana O's words 'Love is the answer, wishes come true, as you remember the place that connects me and you'. Molly looked at the star as she said 'How did she know what I was thinking? How is it that when I am with her anything feels possible? And what was that feeling I had downstairs that told me I needed to get back to my room?' The star continued to glisten in the sky. Molly pulled the blanket more tightly around her, feeling more alone than ever.

As Molly sat there in silence the tears began to flow. She hated everyone being so angry all the time, all the grown-ups getting up in the morning rushing to get out of the door, then when they come home just talking about how rubbish their day has been, then going to bed feeling miserable. 'Is this really how life is supposed to be? Is this the only reason we are here?'

Molly buried her head in her blanket. None of it made sense to her and she just couldn't believe that this was the way life was meant to be. As the tears continued to flow everything went quiet downstairs and then she heard footsteps on the stairs. Molly's head shot up, she flew from behind the curtains back into her bedroom, running across to her bed and diving under the duvet, pulling it right up around her ears so no one could see her, lying perfectly still. Molly heard her bedroom door creak open. 'Molly, are you awake?' she heard her mum whisper. Molly lay motionless holding her breath, trying to pretend she was fast asleep. After a few moments Molly heard the door click close and footsteps going back down the stairs.

She let out a large sigh and then took a big breath in; she still didn't dare open her eyes. As she lay there she carried on thinking about the day she had had at Nana O's and she began to relax, as her body melted into her bed. Just as Molly was about to fall fast asleep she thought she heard an owl hoot just outside her window. She managed a weak smile 'Nan night Nana O' she murmured, and then she was asleep.

The next morning Molly woke to the noise of her parents rushing round the house getting ready for work. As she slowly opened her eyes, allowing them the chance to adjust to the sunlight, her door was pushed open as her mum whirled into the room. 'Molly, come on wake up, we're late, we overslept the alarm clock' Molly's mum said with panic in her voice. Molly felt the cool rush wash over her body as the duvet was pulled back and the weight of her school uniform as they were thrown over her legs.

Molly's mum disappeared out of the bedroom and stomped down the stairs, heading into the kitchen to put on some toast for breakfast. Molly dragged her sleepy body to an upright position and began to peel her pj's off, wishing she could stay asleep where she was having the most incredible dream.

'Come on, Molly, breakfast is ready!' Molly's mum bellowed from the bottom of the stairs just as the door bell rang. Molly's mum spun round and flung the front door open and there stood Molly's best friend Layla. 'She's just coming' Molly's mum said whilst gathering up her things for work.

'Ok' Layla said, confused, wondering where the fire was. 'I'll be down in a minute' a voice called from the top of the stairs. Moments later a more awake Molly came bounding down the stairs, running over to Layla giving her a hug, then grabbing her school coat and the toast her mum was thrusting at her. Layla picked up Molly's school bag by the front door. They were scooted out of the door and into the morning air. Molly shivered as the cool autumn breeze blew and she zipped up her coat.

'Have a great day' Molly's mum said, kissing Molly on the top of her head and dashing to her car. 'Bye, Layla' she said. Layla was about to say bye but the car door was already shut and Molly's mum began to back out of the drive. Molly took the toast she was holding and started nibbling on it as they walked.

As the two girls walked along the path towards school, Layla began to tell Molly what she had been up to over the weekend whilst she watched Molly eating her breakfast. 'You'll never believe what happened, it was the funniest thing I have ever seen' Layla said, flailing her arms around and hitting Molly in the process with Molly's school bag that she was still holding. Molly coughed, grabbing her school bag and flinging it on her shoulder.

'Why, what happened?' Molly asked with a mouthful of toast. 'Dad was trying to fix the garden seat which is next to the pond and as he was pulling on something to try and get it off, it broke and he went flying into the pond. He smelt so bad afterwards, and mum was trying to help him out but couldn't because she was laughing too hard. Me and Amy got it on our phones' Layla said, beginning to chuckle as she relived the memory.

'I thought Amy was at her mum's this weekend?' Molly asked, bewildered. 'She was but they had a big argument and so she came back early. Dad has just kept quiet, he says there is no point jumping into a pit full of angry lionesses' Layla said rolling her eyes.

'Anyway, how was Nana O's?' Layla asked. 'Was it as horrible as you thought it would be? At least it's done now and you don't have to go for another year' Layla said, trying to put a positive spin on it. 'I'm going back tomorrow' Molly said, plunging her hands into her pockets and looking straight ahead, avoiding eye contact with Layla. 'What!' Layla exclaimed, 'All last week you were moaning and moaning and moaning about going to see her. What happened to change your mind?'

They approached the school gates just as the bell rang for the first class. As they walked across the playground they became engulfed in a swarm of the other children who were all heading for the school building. 'Well, it was dead weird' Molly began. 'What was weird?' a familiar voice asked from behind them. They turned round to see Dillon standing there. He moved in closer, draping his arms casually across the two girls' shoulders.

Layla proceeded to push his arm off as if he was a bad, lingering smell. 'Molly actually liked going to see her Nana O and is going again tomorrow' Layla explained. 'What! Seriously?' Dillon said 'after...' 'I know — after all the complaining I did, I get it, but things change' Molly snapped back in anger and stormed into the school building.

Layla and Dillon turned and looked at each other in disbelief. 'What was that all about?' Dillon asked. 'Your guess is as good as mine' Layla replied, looking bewildered. They followed the direction Molly had headed in down the corridor. They reached the classroom door and made their way in for registration. Dillon and Layla pulled an empty chair out as they sat down either side of Molly.

Layla quietly began to take out her books and pencil case. Dillon stared at both of them as they sat in silence. 'Well, I don't mind asking. What the hell was that all about Molly?' Molly didn't reply but continued to stare blankly at the front of the class.

Dillon looked across to Layla for support but Layla just shrugged her shoulders. 'You girls are complicated' Dillon concluded. They heard the classroom door close behind them and the teacher's footsteps make their way to the front of the class, as the lesson began.

Molly looked around the classroom and up at the clock. Only 55 minutes until break. As she looked around at everyone sitting behind their desk listening to the teacher speak, she could hear nothing. Everything looked so out of place, she felt so out of place. Molly glanced back at the clock – 54 minutes to go. She let out a large sigh as her head fell onto her folded arms which were placed on the desk in front of her.

'Is there something wrong?' a voice asked from the front of the room. Molly heard her teacher's footsteps getting closer. Molly slowly lifted her head and began to rub her forehead as thousands of thoughts bounced around in her mind. 'I'm not feeling so good

– could I go outside and get some fresh air?' Molly asked, still staring at the desk.

'Yes, of course, but if you feel unwell you should go and see the school nurse' the teacher said, making her way to the front of the class. Molly couldn't find it in her to even reply. She slowly pushed the chair back, ignoring Layla and Dillon motioning to explain what was wrong, and made her way out of the classroom door.

As she stepped out into the school corridor and closed the door behind her, she leant against the wall and looked up to the ceiling. 'Why do I feel so weird?' Molly said out loud as two children walked past, staring strangely at her.

Molly pushed herself off the wall and made her way back to the playground, where she walked across the playing field to the nearest tree and sat down. Suddenly she let out a sigh of relief. As she felt free once more Molly closed her eyes and her thoughts began to settle down. But then the questions began 'What was that all about? Why did I feel so weird? What really happened at Nana O's?'

Molly opened her eyes and then closed them again, pulling her knees up to her chest. She was suddenly brought back to reality as she felt a hand on her shoulder.

Molly's eyes shot open to see Layla and Dillon crouched down beside her. She then became aware of the noise of children playing, as she looked around the playing field which was now filled with children. Molly looked at Dillon and Layla 'Is it break time already?' Molly stuttered. 'Yep, you were gone for quite some time. The teacher was going to send out a search party' Layla said softly. 'I must have lost track of time' Molly said, looking around and still taking in her surroundings.

'We're worried, Molly. What's up with you? You've been acting really strange' Dillon said, concerned. Molly pulled her body into a seated position as she leant against the tree. She looked at Dillon, than at Layla, both were no longer smiling. 'Something happened when I visited Nana O. I don't understand what it is yet but I just know things have changed. I'm different. It feels like I am remembering something. Nana O said something about me not being ready to receive, but I am now' Molly said, rubbing her eyes, trying to make sense of it all.

'Why? What happened?' Layla said as she sat down, positioning herself by Molly's side. 'You can tell us. We already know you're weird' Dillon said, trying to lighten the mood as he moved round to the other side of Molly. He felt Layla's hand tap him on the back of his head. 'Shut up, Dillon' Layla said protectively.

Molly looked out onto the school playing field,

focusing on the other children running round and playing, oblivious to it all. Molly looked at Layla and then at Dillon who were both sitting there staring at her, their gaze not shifting until she told them both what had happened that weekend at Nana O's.

Molly stared down at her feet. 'It's nothing really' she began. 'Really' Layla said, sarcastically. 'Ok, maybe it was something but I just can't seem to make sense of it, I just have a feeling in my stomach that something bad is going to happen or that something isn't right' Molly said, rubbing her forehead again. 'Well, maybe we can figure out why you feel this way together' Dillon said encouragingly.

As Molly was just about to say the first word, the school bell rang. Molly breathed a sigh of relief. 'We'd best get to class' she said, standing up from under the tree. She gathered her coat and bag that Layla and Dillon had brought out with them. 'Stupid bell' Dillon said in frustration. 'You can tell us the full story at lunch then, Molly' Layla said, determined that whatever was bothering Molly would be known to her by the end of the day. 'Sure, whatever' Molly said, shrugging her shoulders and setting off to walk back to the school building to her next class.

Molly made her way into the school building, heading up the stairs towards her next class when a boy came racing down the stairs. He flew round the corner with one hand on the banister to stop himself from falling forward when he ran head first into Molly. The two of them collided and went flying, as they bashed and bumped down the stairs to the floor.

As they landed in a heap the boy quickly got up, brushed himself down and said "Wake up would ya?" as he took off at a run. Layla and Dillon just stood at the bottom of the stairs in disbelief at what they had just seen. Layla snapped out of her trance and reached down to help Molly to her feet.

'Are you alright?' Layla asked. 'I think so' Molly said, dusting herself off. Dillon stood there looking at them both as his face turned from disbelief to confusion. 'Wake up. That's weird. Normally you would say "sorry" not "wake up"' he said, playing the words over and over again in his mind.

Molly turned and looked at him 'What did you just say?' she asked, now fully alert. 'The boy. The boy who just knocked you flying, he said "Wake up would ya?" Normally you would say sorry or something' Dillon said, staring intently at Molly.

Molly stood there storming at Dillon, becoming annoyed as the anger and confusion of everything filled every cell of her body. She began to think of all the illusions that filled her life, all the lies and deceit.

Molly stormed up the stairs with each footstep sounding like thunder as it echoed around the stairway. Molly marched into class, walking straight past the teacher and to where she would normally sit at the back of the class. She slammed her bag on the table, causing everyone to turn and look at her.

Layla walked in 'I wouldn't mess with her today, someone has just sent her flying down the stairs' she said as she made her way to her seat. The teacher looked up at Molly 'Are you hurt? Do you need to go and see the nurse?' 'I'm fine!' Molly snapped back. The teacher stood tall as he slowly made his way to the door. He turned to look at Molly. 'I think you had better wait outside' he said, pointing outside the classroom door.

'Sir, I haven't done anything wrong' Molly pleaded. 'Just wait outside' the teacher replied. The class fell silent as Molly picked up her school bag and walked between the tables to the classroom door. She continued to look at the floor as she went out into the corridor. The teacher slowly closed the door behind her and Molly listened as she heard the click.

Molly looked up and down the corridor. No one was there. Molly slung her school bag over her shoulder and began to make her way back to the stairs. 'What is the point of sticking around? He won't listen anyway' Molly mumbled to herself.

As she went down the stairs she heard the classroom door above her open. She quickened her pace and just made it outside as she heard the teacher call her name. Molly sprinted across the playground back to the tree she had just been sitting under with Layla and Dillon.

As she reached the tree she leant over, trying to catch her breath. Molly lowered herself to the ground, took off her school bag, leant her back and head against the tree and closed her eyes. She felt a stillness descend over her body as her eyes closed and everything turned black.

As the moments went by, Molly felt her heartbeat and breathing slow down. As she opened her eyes the sun appeared from behind a cloud, showering her in sunlight. Molly let out a sigh; it felt so warm, so safe here. Molly looked around and there was no one to be seen. She took hold of her school bag and opened it, taking out one of her school exercise books and pencil case.

Molly placed the bag down in front of her and opened the book to a blank page, then reaching to take a pen from her pencil case, she began to write.

The words flowed like a river onto the page as she wrote down what had happened at her Nana O's house. The door seemingly opening by itself, the room looking different as Nana O began to tell the story of the locket. As she reached the point where the story began, Molly's pen froze in its position. 'Am

I not just imagining all this?' she whispered to herself. Molly stared at the empty line on the page and then began to write the story.

Molly sat under the tree in the sunshine as the pen flew across the page. She filled each line with words, the story beginning to build line by line, as she retold the story of the locket.

Molly could hear the playing field begin to fill with children once more as class had finished and lunchtime had arrived. Layla and Dillon appeared as they stepped out of the school building, scanning the playing field for Molly. 'There she is' Dillon said, pointing at the tree.

They began to make their way over in silence. 'Hey, what happened? Sir's furious' Layla shouted as they got nearer to where Molly was sitting. Molly didn't look up but continued to write.

'What are you doing?' Dillon asked as they reached Molly and stood looking down at her scribbling as fast as she could onto the pages. Dillon tilted his head to try and read what she was writing upside down. His eyes began to adjust as he focused on the word 'poo'. He said the word aloud and then 'What are you writing?', again trying to hide a giggle inside as he thought about the word poo.

Molly carried on writing, ignoring Dillon's comment. Layla lowered herself to the ground in front of Molly 'You said you were going to tell us what happened at Nana O's' Layla said softly. Layla recalled the memory of the last time she saw Molly acting like this was when her parents had had a huge argument where plates were smashed and the house looked like a war zone.

'I am' were the only words Molly spoke. 'Then tell us' Layla said reassuringly. Molly looked up at Layla and lowered her pen to the ground where it laid in the grass. She handed the book in which she had been writing to Layla. Layla smiled as she took hold of the book and began to flick through the pages to where Molly had begun to write.

Molly leant back against the tree and looked up at the blue sky which had developed as all the clouds had dissolved away whilst she had been writing. 'What does it say?' Dillon asked, just before he took a bite out of his sandwich that he had got out of his bag. Layla looked up from the pages looking at Dillon and then at Molly.

Molly continued to look up at the blue sky. 'It's a story about a locket' Layla said, trying to hide the confusion in her voice. 'Well, go on, read it out' Dillon said with a mouthful of sandwich, some of it flying out of his mouth and landing on the pages. 'That's disgusting, Dillon' Layla said, wiping it off with her sleeve. 'Didn't your parents tell you not to speak with your mouth full?' she said in protest.

'All the time' Dillon smiled, taking another bite. Layla readjusted herself to get comfy and laid the book on her lap. 'It says the story began...' Layla, Dillon and Molly sat under the tree as Layla read out the story of the locket that Molly had heard the day before at Nana O's.

As Layla read out loud the last words 'Love is the answer, wishes come true, as you find the place that connects me and you'. They all sat there silently for a moment contemplating the words. 'What does it mean? Answer to what? Is the locket magical? How did your Nana O know what you were thinking? Is that the end of the story? Do you think this has something to do with the funny feeling you got before you got ploughed down the stairs?' Layla said, reeling question after question off as she sat trying to make sense of it all. 'Now do you see why I have been acting weird all morning?!' Molly said, raising her arms to the sky. 'I get it' Dillon said, now lying on the ground.

Molly and Layla shot him a look of disbelief. 'Out of all of us you get it first' Molly said dismissively. 'It's easy, I can't believe you guys don't get it' Dillon said confidently. Molly and Layla looked at each other as they heard the bell sounding for the end of lunch.

Dillon shot to his feet, grabbing his things and walking with a fast pace across the playing fields. Molly and Layla grabbed their bags. Molly shoved her school exercise book and pencil case back into her bag as she walked, chasing Dillon. 'Aren't you going to tell us?' Layla shouted to Dillon. 'Nope' Dillon replied as he broke out into a run, heading back to the school building.

Molly and Layla started to run, trying to catch Dillon up before he disappeared into his next class. 'Dillon, wait would you' Molly shouted. They heard Dillon begin to laugh as he reached the door and disappeared into the school building.

Molly and Layla finally caught up with Dillon who had already taken his seat in the classroom. Layla and Molly walked across the room and sat at the empty table in front of him. Layla placed her school bag on the table and turned round glaring at Dillon. Neither of them said a word as they continued their staring match, wondering who would break first.

Molly chuckled as she began to take her school exercise book out of her bag. 'Is there a problem, Layla?' the teacher called across the room. Layla swung round in her chair to face the front 'No, Miss'. 'Shall we begin then?' the teacher said, motioning to the board. 'Yes, Miss' Layla said, lowering her school bag to the floor.

'Ha ha, I won' Dillon said with glee as he leant forward across the table. 'Dillon have you got something you wish to share with us?' the teacher asked, beginning to get frustrated with the interruptions. 'No, Miss' he said, leaning back in his chair. Layla turned round to Dillon with a wide grin and stuck out her tongue in jest. Dillon responded by motioning with his hand for her to turn back round to face the front.

Molly was distant again through the whole class but this time she wasn't alone; all three of them sat in total silence as they thought about the story and what the message in the locket meant. "Love is the answer, wishes come true, as you find the place that connects me and you". Molly couldn't concentrate, she just kept doodling in her book as her mind wandered.

Layla looked up at the classroom clock as she watched the hand move closer and closer to break time, 60 seconds, 40 seconds, 25 seconds, ring!, as the bell for break called. Dillon and Layla scooped up their belongings. 'Molly, come on it's break!' Layla said, tapping Molly on the shoulder.

Molly jumped out of her day dream. She turned to look at Layla as she blinked and her eyes began to focus again. 'Where were you?' Dillon said jokily. 'I don't know but it's the same dream I had last night' Molly said as she began to gather her things.

'What dream?' Layla said, curious to see if this was the next clue to the puzzle. They began to walk out of the classroom and into the corridor. As they neared the school building doors they looked out of the window to see dark grey clouds building. They watched them move closer and closer and there was a large rumble of thunder as a storm approached.

'That's odd' Dillon said, staring intently at the storm. 'It was beautiful sunshine and blue sky earlier on'. 'We might as well go and sit in the cafeteria where you can tell us about your dream' Layla said, looking at Molly. 'Can't we just go and sit at the bottom of the stairs?' Molly said, pointing at where she had fallen earlier that day.

They turned and made their way back to the staircase where they settled down on the steps. Dillon and Layla stayed quiet as they waited for Molly to share her dream. 'I know it may sound strange but I saw this storm coming' Molly began, looking out of the window. Layla and Dillon glanced at each other but said nothing.

'In my dream there was a storm whilst we were at school and lightning struck the school building, causing a power failure. They had to send us home early but in front of the storm flew an owl and when I was in the dream I had the same feeling I had last night and this morning' Molly said.

Layla and Dillon looked out of the window and all they could see was the storm gathering momentum, getting closer and closer. 'There's no owl there, Molly' Layla said softly. 'Maybe you're just tired' she said sympathetically. 'No I'm not. I just had the same day dream in class that I dreamt about last night. Of all things I could dream about why the heck would I dream about that?' Molly said, looking down at her hands. 'I'm not crazy you know' Molly said quietly.

'Well, this is the most excitement we have had in months' Dillon said, moving to the edge of the step in eagerness. 'Are you going to tell us what the note in the locket meant now Dillon?' Molly asked sweetly. 'Oh, I haven't the foggiest. I was just making that up to see your two's reaction'. Suddenly he felt Layla's hand tap him on the back of his head again. 'What was that for?' he said, rubbing his head.

'That's for talking rubbish and this is for lying to Molly' as she lifted her hand up. Dillon already knew what was going to happen and ducked his head. 'Maybe Nana O was just making up stories to make the visit more exciting' Molly said, interrupting Layla and Dillon's play fight.

'Her stories have never made you act like this before. I think it means more but if it doesn't it sure makes school more interesting trying to figure it out' Dillon said, getting serious.

They heard the bell ring, signalling the end of break time. They all rose from the steps. As they did, another rumble of thunder roared and a flash of lightning beamed in the distance. They all looked at each other is disbelief. 'It's really far away' Layla said, trying not to freak out. 'I'm not so sure' Dillon said, frozen to the spot.

'We'd best get to class' Molly said, not fazed at all by what was happening but instead feeling pleased that it wasn't just weird things happening with her imagination. Molly made her way into the corridor with Layla and Dillon following behind. As they walked along they could hear the thunder all around as the storm was now over the school.

As they reached the classroom door there was an almighty bang as the corridor lights flickered and then darkness descended. Layla leapt to Dillon's side, wrapping her arms around his waist. 'Oh so now you like me?' he said, wrapping his arms round her to protect her. 'Shut up Dillon' Layla said in fear. Molly stopped in her tracks, looking all around, and said nothing as she walked into the classroom. Through the windows she could see the storm clouds rolling in the sky.

Layla and Dillon quickly followed behind, glad to be out of the dark corridor. They made their way to where Molly was standing staring out of the window. 'I think I might need to get a clean pair of pants'

Dillon said, pretending to cross his legs in fear. The teacher marched through into the classroom, not bothering to close the door, holding a piece of paper in his hand.

'Everyone, can you take your seats, quickly' he said as he moved to the front of the classroom. 'Right, the good news is the lightning only struck the generator; the bad news is you all get to go home early'. The classroom erupted into a cheer!

The teacher began waving his arms to signal for everyone to be silent. 'Hang on, hang on, I've not finished!' he shouted over the cheering. 'The school buses are on their way. If for any reason you can't go home early then you're to head to the hall. For the rest of you we'll see you tomorrow'. The teacher turned on his heels and headed back out of the classroom.

'You can have more of those dreams!' Dillon said, squeezing Molly tight. Molly managed to give a weak smile. 'Do you two want to come back to mine and hang out?' Layla said. Molly nodded her head and started to head out of the classroom. Layla grabbed Dillon's arm as he began to follow Molly. 'Do you know what's going on with Molly?' she whispered. 'Not the foggiest, but I do know Molly needs us more than ever' Dillon said as he turned to walk in the direction of Molly.

Layla jogged to catch up. 'Did I just see a glimpse of your caring side?' Layla said, part sarcastically and part in awe. 'No, it was just your imagination' he said, grinning with enthusiasm. They caught up with Molly who was standing at the door leading to the playing fields. She pulled her hood over her head, 'Ready?' she asked Layla and Dillon. Dillon proceeded to pull his coat zip right to the top, 'Ready!' he said.

Molly pushed open the door and a wave of cool fresh air and lashing rain hit her face. They broke out into a run in the direction of the school gates. As they ran across the playing field, the wet ground squelching under their feet, they reached the pavement where they ran along until they got to the bend in the road.

'Stop! Stop!' Molly and Dillon heard Layla cry from behind. 'It's stopped raining, and I can't run any more' she said, coming to a stop whilst trying to catch her breath. Molly hadn't noticed the rain had stopped and the blue sky had arrived. As they all came to a stop Molly turned round to look back at the school which now had a rainbow across the top of it.

'Look' she said to Layla and Dillon, pointing at the school building. Dillon turned round as Layla came back to an upright position. The three of them stood as they admired the full rainbow before them. 'That's incredible' Dillon said, finally breaking the silence.

They turned and carried on making their way towards Layla's house. None of them spoke as they were trying to figure out the strange coincidences that had been happening all that day.

As they walked round the next corner, Layla's house came into sight. No cars were on the driveway, 'My parents will be back at 6pm, so we have the house to ourselves' Layla said, as she started to fumble through her bag for the door key.

As they walked up the driveway they were greeted by Layla's cat Duke who started to weave through their legs. Layla bent down and scooped him up into her arms. He continued to climb until he was up on her shoulders. 'I'm sure your cat thinks it's a parrot' Dillon said, reaching up and stroking Duke's head as he began to purr.

Layla put the key in the front door, unlocked it and pushed it open. Duke leapt off her shoulder, landed in the hallway and started to make his way to the kitchen. The three of them followed on behind, leaving their school bags by the door as they slipped off their shoes.

They made their way through to the kitchen where Molly sat down at the table. Dillon headed straight for the fridge 'Does anyone else want a snack?' he said with his head inside the fridge. 'Make yourself at home why don't you?' Layla said in jest. 'Don't mind if I do' Dillon replied in a jingle.

'Do you want a cup of tea?' Layla asked, looking at Molly. Molly was just staring out of the patio windows blankly, stroking Duke who had now settled on her lap. 'Molly!' Layla said, but there was still no reply. Dillon took the sandwich he had just been making across to the table where Molly was sitting. As he passed her he waved his hand in front of her face 'Earth to Molly!' he said.

Molly suddenly looked up at Dillon 'Sorry, I was miles away' she said, shuffling in her seat. Duke stood up and circled round before returning to a lying position where he closed his eyes again. 'Tea?' Layla asked, raising up the kettle she was holding in her hand. Molly just nodded.

Molly rested her head on her hand and went back to staring out of the patio window. Layla made her way across to the table with two cups of tea, placing one in front of Molly and one in front of Dillon. Molly wrapped her hands around the warm mug, feeling the warmth travel up through her hands, up her arms and into her heart; it felt like her heart was receiving a hug.

'I'm not going to school tomorrow' Molly said, staring into her tea. Layla came back across with her cup of tea and pulled out a chair opposite Molly. 'What are you going to say to your mum?' Dillon asked through a mouthful of sandwich. 'Dillon!' Layla cried, wiping a piece of cheese off her top that had proceeded to fly out of Dillon's mouth as he spoke.

Dillon chuckled and took another bite. 'I'm going to say I'm not feeling well, it's sort of true, I'm definitely not feeling myself. Then I can go and see Nana O' Molly said, taking a sip of tea and feeling the hug extend from her heart to her whole body.

'Do you think she'll tell you the rest of the story or do you think she will have forgotten? She is pretty old' Dillon said, wiping his mouth with his sleeve. Molly smiled 'She said she isn't old, just wiser, and I want to know how it ends, maybe then we will understand the note in the locket'. 'You must call us as soon as you get back. Better still, we'll come round after school to check you're alright, then you can tell us' Layla said, as her mind continued to formulate a plan.

They all fell back into silence, lost in their thoughts. 'Say the message is true and your Nana O is right and wishes do come true, what would you wish for?' Dillon said. Layla and Molly turned to look at Dillon. 'Wow, Dillon, that was quite an intelligent question. Maybe you're coming down with something too' Layla said sarcastically.

Dillon glared at Layla. 'I don't know. At the moment I think if I could have one wish it would be to understand what this is, the feeling I get when something isn't right, the dream of the storm, it must be connected somehow' Molly said, looking at Layla and Dillon for answers.

'I'd wish for a new bike' Dillon said, slurping his tea, Duke interrupted them with a meow as he stretched out his front legs. 'I think Duke would wish for an endless supply of tuna' Dillon laughed. They all broke out into laughter at the thought of Duke sitting on a mountain made of tins of tuna.

'I think I would wish for unlimited clothes and shopping' Layla said, staring at the ceiling and thinking about all the clothes she could go out and get. 'Then I would have to totally revamp my room because I would need the world's largest wardrobe to put them all in'. Molly began to laugh. 'What's so funny?' Layla asked, as Dillon began to join in laughing too. 'Miss Barbie over there' he said, trying to hold back the giggles, nodding his head towards Layla.

Layla stuck her tongue out at him and reached for her tea. As they sat at the table, Layla and Dillon got lost in their conversation, having a competition of who could come up with the craziest, most outrageous wish. Molly sat listening to the "wish tennis match" between the two of them. She looked down at Duke who lay on her lap. As she began to stroke him her mind relaxed and she felt such warmth and love coming from him.

As the empty cups sat on the table, they heard the front door open. 'Hello!' Layla's mum shouted as she appeared at the kitchen door. 'Oh, hi everyone' she said, lifting the bags of shopping onto the kitchen worktop. 'Hi, mum' Layla said, getting up and walking across to her mum. As she reached her she wrapped her arms around her and her mum bent over and kissed her on her forehead.

'Are you all staying for dinner?' Layla's mum asked, with one arm still wrapped around Layla. 'No, thank you. I'd best be making tracks, I'm not feeling so good' Molly said, getting up from the kitchen table. Duke meowed in protest at being disturbed from his sleep as he jumped from her lap to the floor.

'Oh, do you want some medicine?' Layla's mum asked, concerned. 'No thanks, I'm just going to head home and get an early night' Molly said as she saw Layla give her a wink.

'I'd best be off too otherwise I'll be late for dinner' Dillon said. 'But you have only just eaten!' Layla said in disbelief. 'I'm a growing man' Dillon said patting his stomach. Layla responded by raising her eyebrows at him.

'Very well' Layla's mum said, starting to unpack the shopping. Dillon and Molly made their way to the front door where they put on their shoes and collected their school bags. Layla opened the front door. As they looked out they saw the sun beginning to set on the horizon as dusk arrived. 'See you tomorrow' Layla said, hugging Molly. 'Yep' Molly replied quickly and made her way outside.

Dillon moved in for a hug. 'No chance' Layla said, pushing him out of the door. Dillon pretended to look sad. 'Bye, Dillon' Layla said playfully as she closed the front door. Molly and Dillon walked down the driveway. As they reached the road Molly slowed down 'See you tomorrow' she said, giving Dillon a hug. 'You betcha' Dillon said as he squeezed her. They set off in opposite directions back home. Molly walked as the blanket of the night sky followed the setting sun. Molly let out a groan as the tiredness of the day set in. As she crossed the road she looked up to see her house there in front of her. She turned and looked back, realising she had been in a day dream the whole way home, not remembering getting there.

She made her way up to the front door. As she turned the handle and made her way in she threw her school bag on the floor, heading straight upstairs to her room. Her mum and dad watched her from the living room. 'Are you alright, Molly?' Molly's dad asked. 'I'm not feeling well so I'm going to bed, see you in the morning' she said quietly and disappeared upstairs.

As Molly reached her bedroom she flopped on her bed and groaned again as she pulled her duvet up over her, disappearing from sight. She listened as she heard footsteps up the stairs. 'Please just leave me alone' Molly began to repeat to herself.

Molly heard the footsteps walk across the landing and into her room as the floorboards creaked. Then she heard the rings from her curtains slide across the curtain pole. The footsteps became louder as they neared where she was lying.

She felt a kiss on the top of her head. 'Night' her dad said, then turned and made his way out of her bedroom, closing the door behind him. Molly listened as the footsteps got fainter and her eyelids got heavier. Sleep finally took over her body and she drifted off into the land of dreams.

4 THE TALE BECOMING MORE THAN A STORY

Molly was awoken the next day by her dad roaring at her mum as they argued downstairs. Their piercing shouts travelled up the stairs and filled Molly's room with an intense cold feeling. She felt her body absorb the anger like poison as she pulled the duvet up over her head to blank out her mum retaliating by shouting back.

'Please make them stop shouting, please make them stop shouting' Molly repeated over and over again to herself. Molly suddenly felt a whoosh of cool air over her. She threw back her duvet and went over to the window, drawing back the curtains. 'That's weird, the window isn't even open' she said. Her gaze shifted to take in the beautiful autumn day outside. She opened the window and stuck her head outside.

As she breathed in the crisp fresh air, she no longer felt trapped; she felt she could breathe again. Molly took in another deep breath of air, feeling her body relax even more, letting out all the anger that had been floating around the room which had then been absorbed by her.

Molly closed her eyes and leant her head against the window frame. She didn't want to go downstairs, she didn't want to see her parents in all their rage. Molly's eyes shot open, 'Nana O' she said passionately. Molly began to hear footsteps coming up the stairs; she darted across to her bed and dived in, pulling the duvet up around her neck.

As she closed her eyes pretending to be asleep, her bedroom door creaked open. 'Molly, are you awake?' her mum's voice said. There was a slam of the front door as her dad stormed out of the house. Molly began to move under the duvet, trying to look like she had just woken up.

As Molly opened her eyes and stretched her arms above her head, her mum moved across and sat down on the edge of her bed. 'How are you feeling today love?' her mum enquired, stroking Molly's hair. 'Any better?' she asked. Molly rolled over towards her mum, scrunching up into a ball and slowly shook her head.

Molly's mum placed her hand on Molly's forehead. 'You haven't got a temperature' she said as she continued to inspect Molly. 'It's my stomach, I must have eaten something yesterday at lunch' Molly said as she rubbed her stomach. Molly's mum looked out of the window, 'It's just that I can't leave you here on your own and I need to go and see your Nana today'.

Molly pulled herself into a sitting position and wrapped her duvet tightly around herself. 'That's ok, mum, I can just come with you and lie on Nana O's sofa whilst you do your jobs' Molly said, looking straight into her mum's eyes. 'I'm going to Nana O's, I'm going to Nana O's', Molly whirled the words around in her head.

As they sat in silence as her mum contemplated what to do, they heard a knock at the door. Molly's mum got up from the bed without saying a word and made her way down the stairs to the front door. Molly listened intently as she heard a familiar voice. It was Layla's voice. 'Is Molly ready?' she heard Layla ask.

'I'm afraid she isn't coming to school today. She seems to have picked up a stomach bug, she thinks from something she ate yesterday' Molly's mum replied, looking behind her up the stairs. 'Oh, ok, no problem. I'll call round after school to see how she is doing' Layla said whilst trying to keep a straight face.

'I think it's best if you wait until tomorrow and let her rest' Molly's mum said sympathetically. 'But, I need to...' Layla began, knowing she couldn't wait until tomorrow to hear the rest of the story. 'Tomorrow, Layla' Molly's mum said a bit firmer. Layla shuffled on the spot. 'Can you tell her I said hi' Layla said uncomfortably. 'Will do' Molly's mum replied as she began to slowly close the door.

Molly heard the front door close shut and raised her hands to the sky in celebration 'YES!' Molly quickly wrapped the duvet around herself and continued the act of feeling ill as she heard her mum returning up the stairs. Molly's mum poked her head round the door, 'Ok, you'll have to come with me and lie on Nana O's sofa and I'll try and be as quick as I can' Molly's mum said before disappearing into her own room to get ready.

Molly shuffled from side to side, jiggling her bum in excitement. She rolled out of bed, found her jumper and put it on over her pj's. She then put on her socks. She grabbed the blanket that was lying at the end of the bed. As she looked at it, remembering that it was the blanket her Nana had given her as a baby, Molly stopped and sat down at the bottom of her bed.

As she let the blanket slip through her fingers she saw all the different colours, the patterns seemed so much brighter. She realised that she had never really looked at the blanket before and for a long time she even hated it, but now it felt safe, it felt warm. As Molly swung it over her shoulders and wrapped it around her body, it felt like home.

She sat there on the end of the bed smiling to herself.

Who would have known? Her mum entered her bedroom, interrupting Molly's thoughts. 'Ready?' Molly's mum said, motioning to head downstairs. 'I'm ready' Molly said as she raised herself up from the bed with the blanket draped down her back.

She walked past her mum with pride. Her mum watched Molly walk by and frowned as Molly looked far from ill right now. Molly made her way down the stairs to the front door where she slipped on her shoes and stood staring at the door.

Molly's mum whirled past her, grabbed her handbag off the bottom step, lifted the keys off the hook and opened the front door. Molly stood staring for a moment at the open door. 'Same door, different me' she thought as she took her first step outside.

Molly made her way to the back of the car, waiting for the door to be unlocked. As Molly's mum finished locking the front door, Molly watched as the car lights flashed as her mum unlocked the car. Molly opened up the back door of the car and slid onto the seat, closing the door behind, enjoying getting out of the angry atmosphere that still lingered in the house.

She watched her mum walk across towards the car, open the driver's door and get in. As her mum slid the key into the ignition she looked at Molly through the rear view mirror. 'Good job you are actually ill because I could get into a whole lot of trouble if you were just missing school' Molly's mum said coldly, her eyes carrying on their interrogation.

'Absolutely, I'm definitely not feeling myself' Molly said, staring back at her mum with the same intent. 'Hhmm' her mum concluded as she started the car and reversed back off the driveway.

Not a word was said as the buildings began to fade and were replaced with rolling hills and trees. Molly began to enjoy seeing the grass and hedgerows instead of pavements and fences. 'What were you and dad arguing about this morning?' Molly asked, not taking her eyes off the view out of the window. 'Oh, nothing for you to worry about' Molly's mum said as her grip became tighter around the steering wheel.

Molly's mum reached across and turned on the radio. She turned it up a little louder in an effort to drown out the noise of her thoughts and stop any more questions. Molly looked across at her mum's reflection in the rear view mirror and saw the lines of pain across her face.

Molly looked away, readjusted herself in the seat and pulled the blanket that still lay across her shoulders around her body more tightly. She went back to looking out of the window. In the distance Molly saw the single tree that always signalled that they were close to Nana O's.

The car flung from one side of the road to the other as her mum took the corners with speed, knowing every single bend and turn with clarity. Molly reached across, taking hold of the car door handle to stop herself being flung around the back of the car again. 'I'm sure this happened last time' Molly said, remembering the last time that they came to see Nana O. 'What did you say?' Molly's mum grunted, keeping her eyes glued to the road.

'Nothing, just talking to myself' Molly said distantly. There was no response from her mum. Nana O's cottage came into sight. Molly let out a sigh of relief as the car took another sharp corner, throwing Molly into the door. The car sped up and then came to a screeching halt. Molly looked across to the cottage and there stood in the doorway was Nana O.

Molly's mum turned off the ignition, got out of the car and slammed the door. 'Why does mum get so angry when she comes here?' Molly said aloud to herself in the car. She watched as her mum stomped her way up the garden path and began speaking to Nana O. Nana O started to nod her head and then stepped to one side, allowing Molly's mum to pass her by into the house.

Nana O turned back to looking at the car. 'Are you coming in or letting me grow old on this door step?' Nana O chimed. Molly quickly unbuckled her belt and opened the car door, sliding down, her feet hit the ground with a thump as she closed the car door behind her. She made her way up to where Nana O was standing.

'I hear you're sick' Nana O, said raising her eyebrows.
'Yes, I think I ate something funny yesterday' Molly responded, placing her hands on her stomach.
'Really? Hhmm … or you're just not digesting your experiences very well, if you hold onto something that isn't good for you then you will become sick' Nana O said, placing her hands in front of her.

Molly stopped and looked up at Nana O with confusion. 'What do you mean?' Molly said. 'I'll go and make us a pot of tea as your mum has instructed me that you are to lay on the sofa and sleep' Nana O said as her eyes twinkled with mischief.

Molly followed Nana O into the house. As Nana O turned into the kitchen, Molly went in the opposite direction into the living room, where the fire was already lit and blazing out heat. Molly looked around the room and saw the furniture had been rearranged. The sofa had been moved and was now opposite the chair Nana O sat in.

'How did she know?' Molly said to herself as she made her way across the room to sit down on the sofa on the side closest to the fire. Molly readjusted her blanket and a few cushions as she got herself comfy.

Nana O appeared at the living room door holding a tray with a teapot, two cups and a plate of biscuits. She slowly shuffled her way across the living room, taking great care not to spill any tea, and placed the tray down on the small table beside her chair.

She lifted the teapot and began to pour. Molly watched but instead of the usual brown liquid coming out it was a green colour with bits in it. 'I thought we were having tea?' Molly asked, wrinkling her nose at the sight before her. 'We are' Nana O said, handing Molly one of the cups. Molly looked down at the contents inside the cup. 'You said you had eaten something funny and this will help to settle your stomach' Nana O said with a cheeky smile.

'Why do I get the feeling that this is payback for lying?' Molly said, sniffing the green coloured water. 'Ah, life will always keep the balance and it would do you well to remember that what you give out, you will receive' Nana O said, slowly lowering herself into her seat and ending with a thud as her bum hit the chair.

Nana O lifted her cup. Molly noticed that hers was normal tea. Nana O took a sip and watched Molly's face of disapproval. 'I'm not the one with the poorly stomach, remember' Nana O said as she chuckled. Molly lifted the cup to her lips and took a sip. Her face screwed up in disgust, 'Umm, lovely' she replied sarcastically, placing the cup down on the table beside her.

Nana O leant back in her chair in satisfaction, 'Not many people like the taste of lies'. Nana O began to lean forward to get a better look at the blanket wrapped around Molly. 'And there's me thinking you got rid of that' Nana O said, admiring the beauty of the intricate design on the blanket.

Molly glanced down, pulling the blanket further around her. 'No. I saw it at the end of my bed and had a strange feeling that I should bring it with me, so I did' Molly said, not taking her eyes off the blanket.

'How interesting' Nana O said, placing her hands on her lap. 'And do you often get these feelings and, most of all, do you follow them?' Nana O asked. 'It's funny you should say that. Something really strange happened at school yesterday. I had a day dream that something would happen and then it did' Molly said, thinking back to yesterday. 'I was kind of hoping you would be able to explain to me what is happening' Molly said, looking intently at Nana O.

'How perfect' is all Nana O said, as she fell silent and gazed into the fire. Molly listened as she heard the birds outside chirping. 'Very well' Nana O said, breaking the silence. 'Shall we continue with our story?' she asked as she threw another log onto the fire and returned to leaning back in her chair.

'Will you answer my question?' Molly asked. 'I think you will find the answer in the story, it's not always a case of learning something new, it's about remembering something you had forgotten was true' Nana O said with a smile.

'Where were we up to?' Nana O said, tapping her fingers on the chair arm. 'Ah, yes, he was sitting at the kitchen table, humming his tune "love is the answer, wishes come true, as you remember the place that connects me and you"' Nana O said quietly to herself.

Nana O let out a sigh. As Molly watched her eyes become brighter, her face looked less wrinkled and the room seemed to come to life. 'That evening, as he made his way to bed, he saw his reflection in the mirror, and instead of the disappointment he usually felt towards the person staring back at him, he felt love. He shook his head at the bizarre feeling that came from deep within, and got undressed, slipped under the duvet and was promptly joined by his wife. She reached across and turned off her bedside light and the room descended into darkness.

Moments later, Jacob heard his wife snoring in the background. He stared up at the ceiling in the dark, as his mind continued to chatter about all that had happened that day. He then paused as a thought passed through his mind. 'What would I wish for if it were to come true? What is it that I truly want?' His mind suddenly went blank. He had been so busy noticing how things had been going wrong that he had never given a second thought to what he actually wanted instead. 'They say the day is a gift' he whispered to himself. 'Well, the gift I will receive tomorrow is to be happy at work'. His mind began to drift to how much he hated work and how much he hated his boss, and his old conversation began once more. As he lay there he found himself starting to hum, interrupting the chatter by the little song he had created that evening: 'love is the answer, wishes come true, as you remember the place that connects me and you'.

He paused for a moment. 'So love makes wishes come true. No, that can't be right' he thought. 'I love so many people and that hasn't made my life any better'. He rolled over and picked up his phone, trying to distract himself from his thoughts. As he scrolled through the latest news, a headline in big, bold letters appeared: THEY FOUND THE PLACE WHERE ALL IS LOVED UNCONDITIONALLY. But as he clicked on the headline to read the article, an error message appeared.

How weird he said in confusion. His wife grumbled in the background and he quickly turned off his phone. 'What place? There is no place on this planet where that is true' he thought as he rubbed his forehead. He rolled onto his side and closed his eyes. As his eyes shut he saw the locket in his imagination. 'I'd best return that' he mumbled as his mind fell silent as he finally went to sleep.

Molly had curled up in a ball on the sofa, staring intently at Nana O. 'I know that place you're talking about – I went there in my dreams' Molly said. 'Now, now, don't you go getting ahead of the story' Nana O said with such joy as she watched Molly begin to remember one of life's truths.

Nana O continued 'Jacob was woken up in the usual way as the children whirled into the bedroom, jumped on the bed and climbed under the duvet. He rolled over to be greeted with a wide grin from his daughter. 'Morning!' she cheered, with his son's head popping up from behind. 'Morning you lovely monsters' he replied as he started the day with the intention he had set the night before.

The house transformed into organised chaos as they all got ready for work and school. Jacob managed to escape as the children were busy eating their breakfast and his wife was putting the packed lunches into their school bags. As he made his way round the room giving each one a kiss, wishing them a lovely day, he reached the back door where he was greeted by their dog.

The dog proceeded to bounce around the room with excitement, acting like it was the first time he had seen him in ages. The man reached for his jacket, slipped it on and slid his hand into the pocket where his fingers touched the locket. This caused him to smile as his body felt the same warm feeling he got last night. He took the dog's lead off the hook and placed it in his other pocket. As he reached for the door handle he saw his own reflection in the glass. 'I may not love you yet but at least we're now heading in the right direction' he said to himself and opened the door, stepping out into the fresh spring air.

As he made his way down the side of the house, through the gate out to his car with his dog in tow, he started to hum again, with his footsteps beating out the rhythm. As he reached his car the dog whipped round to the boot where he sat in eager anticipation. The man followed him round, opened it up and the dog leapt inside.

'If only I could be more like you: happy and full of energy and life' he said as he ruffled the dog's fur. He then closed the car boot, made his way round to the driver's side and got in. As the car came to life he let out a sigh and sat staring at the house. He began to chuckle to himself at the absurdity of the last 24 hours, ever since he found… He began to connect the dots.

'Since I found the locket…' he said to himself, reaching into his pocket and pulling the locket out. He stared at it dangling in front of him. He shook his head in disbelief. 'That's only make-believe, fairy tale stuff, it doesn't actually come true' he mused to himself. Just then the locket caught the sunlight and appeared to shine brightly. 'Or does it?' he questioned.

He was interrupted from his thoughts as he heard the front door slam and saw his wife and children begin to make their way to the car. He quickly slipped the locket back into his pocket and put the car into reverse. As he backed off the driveway and set off down the road he turned the radio on and attempted to drown out his thoughts and all the questions he had whirling around in his head.

Jacob continued driving to work. Looking out of the window he pulled up at the first set of traffic lights. He started to slow down; he watched as they turned from amber to green. He began to drive forward again. As he took the next turning to the right he made his way down the road, approaching the next set of traffic lights which then again changed from red to amber to green as he approached them. He stared confused at the traffic lights as he passed them.

'It must just be a coincidence' he said to himself. He continued down the road to the next set of traffic lights and the same happened again. 'What is going on!' he exclaimed, looking in his rear view mirror at the dog. 'This never, ever happens!' As he continued to make his way to work every set of traffic lights did the same. He pulled into the car park and found his usual spot. He turned off the ignition and sat in silence.

He turned in his seat to look back at his dog. 'Did you do that?' he asked. The dog just tilted his head to the side in response. He turned back in his seat and continued to stare out of the car window. 'That wasn't just coincidence: eight traffic lights all on green. That was amazing!' he yelled, raising his hands up above his head in celebration.

He opened the door, hopped out of the car and made his way round to let the dog out of the boot. As he closed the boot door he looked around the car park. 'This is the same car park' he thought, 'But I feel different; how is it that yesterday I dreaded this car park but today I love it?' Jacob looked down at his dog sitting in front of him. 'Strange. This is all very strange' and with that he began to make his way into the reception.

As he opened the door, his dog ran to the lady sitting behind the reception desk. She knelt down, giving him scratches, and pulled out a dog treat from her pocket. 'I really love how you do that' Jacob said as he watched them. The lady's head shot up in surprise. 'Oh, umm, thank you' she stuttered. He smiled and continued to make his way through the reception to the back to his office. Jacob's dog slowly moved away from the lady as he was hoping for another treat. But then he bounded into the office where Jacob was just hanging up his coat.

Jacob made his way round to his desk where he

started up his computer and the dog laid on his bed by the window. As Jacob was reaching for the papers from yesterday, there was a knock at his door. 'Come in' he called. The door swung open and there stood his boss.

Jacob felt all the life drain out of his body as his boss moved towards him and towered over him. He began to reel off all that needed to be done, all that he hadn't done, and most of all, all the mistakes he had made. Jacob sat in silence and felt his body temperature rise as his blood began to boil with rage and anger. He continued to sit motionless, receiving the wrath of his boss. There was a call from down the hall and Jacob's boss paused to listen. Without another word the boss spun on his heels and was out the door.

Jacob gingerly got up from behind his desk, feeling lifeless, and made his way to the door, slowly closing it. As the door clicked closed he looked at the dog. 'Why is it that when I'm just beginning to get things right the vampire appears and sucks all life and happiness from me?'

Jacob made his way back to the desk and flopped in his chair, continuing to stare at the door. 'There is nothing to like about him' he said through gritted teeth. The dog barked in response and made his way to his coat, nudging it with his nose. Jacob looked with scepticism. 'Love is the answer, wishes come true, as you remember the place that connects me and you' he repeated to himself, thinking about the locket. 'If there was only a way I could find one thing to like about him then I could wish him away' he said. He suddenly began to laugh as he pictured his boss as a strange cartoon vampire going round everyone sucking out their happiness. His laugh grew louder and louder until tears streamed down his cheeks.

There was another knock at the door. He started to motion for the person to enter as he wasn't able to speak between his fits of laughter. After a few moments he began to compose himself. 'Come in' he said, and his boss was standing in the doorway. Jacob couldn't help himself as he started to roar with laughter again at the sight of him. The boss stood there confused and then became annoyed. 'Well, whatever you're finding funny you are needed in the conference room. I have called a meeting'. The boss took another look at the man sitting laughing in front of him whilst nodding his head in acknowledgement.

The boss did his usual spin on his heels and stormed down the corridor. The laughter began to fade as Jacob tried not to bring the picture back into his imagination of his boss as a vampire. He looked at the open door and then down at the desk as he thought 'I feel great, he didn't bother me this time'. He rose up out of his seat and made his way out of the door, letting out a chuckle here and there as he went.

As he reached the conference room he was greeted by all the staff, some sitting and the rest standing around the edge of the room. Jacob made his way in, squeezing past a few of his colleagues and then standing next to the receptionist. 'Why are we all here?' he asked her. 'Well, rumour has it that the boss has got a transfer and is moving'. Jacob froze, 'When did this happen?' he asked her in astonishment. 'The call came through this morning' she said in a hushed voice.

'This morning' he repeated to himself. The boss appeared at the entrance to the conference room and everyone parted like the red sea as he made his way to the front of the room. He coughed and cleared his throat as silence descended in the room. 'Some of you may know why you're here', a few heads turned to look at each other in the room, trying to decipher who did and didn't know, 'And that I have had my transfer accepted. The reason I am moving is not because of the reasons you may all think, but for personal matters. Your new boss will be here tomorrow'. With that the boss marched out of the conference room back to his office.

The room erupted in noise as questions bounced around the room. 'Who is the new boss? Are they nice? Anyone is nicer than him', it continued. Jacob just stood frozen to the spot, not believing what he had just heard. Without saying anything he made his way out of the conference room back to his office, to be greeted by his dog wagging his tail eagerly.

Jacob knelt down. 'You'll never believe what's just happened! He has only gone and left!' Jacob said as he began to dance around the room with his dog. He danced his way over to his desk and flopped on the chair, looking out of the open door, watching everyone come and go, speaking in whispers.

As they bounced around ideas, what ifs and what's to come, he paid little attention to the pile of papers that sat dormant on his desk. He cupped his head with his hands, as his mind began to wander. 'That locket has done something to me' he thought, bewildered.

He pulled open his desk drawer and took out a note book. He took hold of the pen that was already on his desk and began to write: 'love is the answer, wishes come true, as you remember the place that connects me and you'.

He looked blankly at the words before him. 'How can 17 words change my whole life around?' he thought, putting the pen down.

He looked across and pulled his computer keyboard and mouse closer to him. As he moved the mouse the computer came alive. He clicked on the internet and proceeded to write in the search box 'love is the answer, wishes come true, as you remember the place that connects me and you'. After clicking search the computer began to display pages and pages of answers.

As he read through the different titles he clicked on the third suggestion in the list. As the page appeared, with a background of stars, he began to read. 'Amongst all the legends the one least understood is the universal law of oneness', he murmured as he read aloud to himself. 'To know oneself is to know everything, we are not separate as some might believe. We may have our own way about ourselves but our essence is all one of the same. To truly know life and thus know yourself you seek and connect with that essence inside, and as you do you will remember your ability to be able to create it into anything you like. However, this can only be done from a place of love, as only then is life's flow restored as you have enough energy to create worlds'.

He sat back in his seat staring at the computer screen and then he went across to his jacket where the locket lay in his pocket. 'It can't be that simple. I found the locket which helped me to remember to love and, whoosh, my wishes start to come true' he mused.

His gaze shifted to looking at the open door, remembering what had just happened with his boss. 'Well, alright then, I wish for a new sports car, silver, with a soft top, and what I love about the car I already have is that it is always reliable and good in all weathers', the man then sat and waited, and waited some more.

Nothing happened. 'See, I knew it was a load of rubbish', he mumbled to himself, and picked up one of the pieces of paper from the pile on his desk and clicked open a document on his computer and began to type.

As the noise of his fingers clicking on the keyboard filled the room, he heard the voice of a little boy running around the corridors making pretend racing car noises. He looked up to see the little boy run into his office, chasing around in circles with something in his hand.

The boy then became distracted when he spotted the dog, dropped the object in his hand, ran over to where the dog was lying and began to scratch his belly. Then he heard his mum call from down the corridor and sprung up, stumbling as he ran out of the room.

The man blinked in disbelief and then something caught his eye. He pushed his chair away from his desk and walked towards where the object was. As he knelt down and picked it up, 'Seriously' he said aloud and there in his hand was a toy silver soft top sports car. He looked at his dog, 'I think someone is having a laugh with me' he said.

Making his way back round to his desk, he placed the car in front of his computer screen. He sat at his desk for the rest of the afternoon, typing away on his computer and working his way through his job list. Every now and then he looked at the silver sports car toy and chuckled to himself.

As he filed the last piece of paper away and closed down his computer, he picked up the toy car and held it in his hands. 'I guess it doesn't really matter if every wish I make comes true because it sure has been one of the best days ever just thinking about it and not being so frustrated and angry' Jacob said to himself.

He put the car back down on the desk on top of the notepad where he had written 'love is the answer, wishes come true, as you remember the place that connects me and you'. He then made his way over to where his coat was hung and slipped it on as his dog watched eagerly and then sprung into action, sprinting across to the doorway.

'Yes, yes, it's time to take you for your walk' Jacob said, sauntering over to where the dog was waiting. They walked out into the corridor and he reached for the door and closed it behind him. He walked down the corridor and began to whistle to himself, into the reception area he went, where his dog bounced over to the reception lady who was already waiting for him with a treat in her hand. The dog devoured the treat. 'See you tomorrow' Jacob said, nodding his head. The lady just waved politely and went back behind her desk

'Come on, you, time to head to the fields' he said, pushing the entrance door open so the dog could scoot through the small gap. Jacob walked across the car park and the car lights flashed as he unlocked it. He reached to open up the boot and the dog jumped in and lay down.

The man lowered the boot door, closing it with a click. He walked around to the driver's side and got in. He put the key in the ignition and the car started up straight away. 'I sure do love this car' he said to himself, beginning to laugh at the quirk of fate.

He reversed out of the space and began to head to the place where they walked each evening. This time he had a little less luck with the traffic lights as he watched them change from green to red. 'That's fine with me, I'm in no rush' he said, staring out the windscreen.

He drove in a day dream as his mind meandered through the day and he mused about how much had changed in such a short space of time. It hadn't been hard, if anything it could be said that it had been quite enjoyable. 'Huh' he said aloud as he thought about it. He began to slow the car down as he reached the turning in the road to head into the car park. He pulled into his usual spot and turned the ignition off.

The dog shuffled in the boot with excitement, recognising where they were. Jacob watched him in the rear view mirror, 'Come on then, I bet you're bursting for a wee!'. Jacob opened his door. Whilst climbing out of the car his body felt so relaxed as he pushed the door closed and walked round to the boot of the car. Just as the boot was opening the dog leapt out and disappeared off into the undergrowth.

'I guess you were desperate' Jacob said, closing the boot shut and following in the direction his dog had gone. As he walked along the path, enjoying another spring evening looking at the trees beginning to bud, he slipped his hand into his jacket pocket. He felt the locket between his fingers which caused him to smile to himself.

He took his hand out and let it flop by his side as he continued on his walk. He watched his dog bounce around, darting from one side of the path to the other, sniffing all the different smells.

Jacob began to make his way down the hill back to the car park, remembering the day before when he fell in the mud and how unhappy he had been. 'Well, I am definitely not that person today' he said delightedly as he stepped over the puddle. He continued down the path until he reached the gate at the bottom which opened out onto the car park. His dog was already waiting.

Jacob walked through the gate into the car park and reached into his pocket where the locket had been. He felt nothing. He looked down as he opened up his pocket wider and peered in. It was empty. He then shuffled around the spot where he stood to see if it had fallen out of his pocket. Still nothing. He turned to look up at the hill he had just come down. 'Well, I guess I've learnt my lesson, I hope it helps someone else like it has helped me'. He opened the gate and made his way back to the car.

Nana O let out a large sigh. 'Oh come on Nana O, there must be more to the story' Molly pleaded. 'Oh there are plenty of stories and plenty of lessons, but that'll do for today. You're meant to be ill, remember?' Nana O smiled cheekily.

Molly wiggled back amongst the cushions she had gathered around herself, 'I guess'. 'But I have a feeling that you have questions' Nana O said, intertwining her fingers on her lap.

5 WORDS AND WISHES

'When are you going to stop telling those stupid stories?!' a harsh voice said from the doorway. Nana O and Molly looked across the room to see Molly's mum standing leaning against the doorway. 'I told you to let her sleep. She is supposed to be sick' she said with venom. 'You know full well these are not stupid stories. They are wisdom and truths that have been passed from generation to generation for years. Do you not remember this story?' Nana O said passively. 'I do and I also remember for years believing that rubbish and it did jack buggery for my life!' Molly's mum shouted. She took a deep breath in, fuelling the fire raging in her stomach. 'I will ban Molly from coming here if you keep filling her head with these fairy tales saying that wishes come true!' she yelled.

'Now, now' Nana O said, sitting still and silent, allowing Molly's mum's outrage to pass through her. 'Do you not remember that little green book you kept?' Nana O said, getting up from her chair and making her way over to the bookcase in the corner of the room. Molly's mum's face turned to thunder. 'I threw that away' she said through gritted teeth. 'Oh, I know you did love, and I brought it back again' Nana O said blissfully. 'Ah, here we go' she said, lifting a small green tatty book off the shelf, as she shuffled back to her chair, plonking herself in it, and opened up the book.

'Don't you dare think about reading one word from that book!' Molly's mum marched over as she went to snatch the book out of Nana O's hand. Nana O lifted it just out of reach from her grasp. 'I may be old darling but I'm not dead yet' Nana O said and tucked the book under her bum.

'Why are you so childish?!' Molly's mum screamed. She turned to Molly 'We are going' Molly's mum said as she glared at her. 'I'm not going' Molly replied meekly as she pulled the blanket round her shoulders more tightly. 'This isn't up for discussion young lady' Molly's mum said as she stormed out into the hallway to get her things. Molly looked across at Nana O for help. 'You can collect her in the morning, she'll be fine staying here for the night with me, anyway, she is already dressed in her pj's' Nana O said. Even though her voice hadn't got any louder there was a strength in her words and an undertone that meant this wasn't up for discussion either.

Molly's mum made her way to the door and, looking at both of them sitting by the fire, spun around and slammed the front door behind her as she went. Molly and Nana O continued to sit in silence as they heard the car gears grind and the car roar at speed down the lane.

The atmosphere returned to its usual peaceful state. Molly let out a large sigh 'I hate it so much when she gets angry'. 'Well, I'm sure your mum isn't the only angry person you're going to meet in your life' Nana O began. 'How do you handle it so well? It's like I was watching you dissolve away her anger' Molly said, staring intently at Nana O. 'You turn into the essence of the wind. You can't push on the wind, no matter how much you try by kicking and screaming' Nana O said graciously.

'Don't be daft, Nana O, you can't turn yourself into the wind' Molly said smiling. She thought that her Nana O really had gone crazy. 'Yes you can but first you need to know what anger is'. She reached under her bum to retrieve the green book as it started to indent in her bottom. 'Imagine every feeling we have is like a glass of water. When you feel the happy feelings, the glass fills up with more water. When you feel the sad feelings, the glass empties. Now sometimes it's important to empty your glass because of certain experiences. For this purpose we will say that a fly lands in your water and you need to empty the glass to get rid of the fly before it starts to disintegrate and make the water toxic which then causes you to get ill. But then you have to fill up your glass again with water through the happy feelings. But with anger it's like someone taking the water in your glass and tipping it into theirs. This may be because they are unable to fill up their own glass so they go around taking other people's water' Nana O said, giving Molly a sideways glance to see if she was still following.

'So how is it that mum didn't stick around when she was shouting at you? Mum and dad's arguments sometimes last for hours' Molly said as she shivered at the memories. 'That's because when they are arguing they keep stealing each other's water to fill their empty glass and don't want to be the one left with an empty glass' Nana O continued. 'I guess that makes sense' Molly thought as she felt a part of her understand that it rang some truth. 'So how do you stop people from stealing the water from your glass?' Molly asked. 'Well, there are three ways. The first you already know: turn into the essence of the wind, don't join in, let the words flow through you and out the other side. Second: share your water if you have a continuous flow filling up your cup by looking around you and finding things you love. Most of all you can say thank you for having different things in your life: that's the simplest. Third and my personal favourite: put a lid on your glass by imagining a bubble around you that nothing but love can pass through, and watch how quickly the person turns and walks away because they are getting nothing from you. But listen carefully Molly. They are angry for a reason so you still need to resolve what it is that created the situation in the first place' Nana O said, emphasising her words.

Molly shuffled in her seat as she felt uncomfortable with the last bit. 'Is there no way of just avoiding it in the first place?' Molly said, looking at her feet. Nana O erupted into laughter as she was once again set off into a fit of chuckles. Molly smiled and began to chuckle herself at her Nana's infectious laugh. They both sat there as each time one of them began to regain composure the other one would set them off again.

Eventually Molly was the first to get control of her giggles, slowly returning back to normal. She sat waiting for Nana O to join her. 'Oh Molly' Nana O said with glee. 'Life would be pretty bland if there wasn't a bit of variety, some zest, some spiciness thrown in from time to time'. 'I guess' Molly replied, smiling at the thought.

'Well, we'd best make a start on dinner' Nana O said, getting up from her chair. 'You go and fill up the basket with logs; I have a feeling we'll be needing them tonight' Nana O said as she handed Molly the basket. Molly let out a groan at the thought of going back into the shed.

Molly shrugged off the blanket and it flopped onto the sofa. She made her way across the living room towards the front door. As Nana O heard the front door close she moved across to the sofa where the blanket lay. She reached and picked it up, bringing it closer to her heart. 'I was wondering when you would make your appearance' she said as she lay the blanket back down on the sofa.

Nana O took hold of the sofa arm as she shuffled across the living room and headed into the kitchen where Molly's mum had left out a pot of stew and some potatoes for dinner. Nana O took the potatoes to the sink where she proceeded to fill the pan with water. She stared out of the kitchen window watching Molly dragging the basket of logs across the ground, having to keep stopping as the logs tumbled off the top of the basket.

She listened as she heard Molly grunt and groan as she brought the basket through the front door and into the living room, letting out a large sigh when she had reached the fire. Molly meandered into the kitchen, pulled out one of the kitchen chairs and sat at the table.

Nana O lifted the pot of peeled and chopped potatoes, put them on the cooker and turned on the hob. 'What's for dinner?' Molly asked, staring at the large pot of potatoes. 'Stew' Nana O said, pulling out a chair to join Molly at the table. They sat in silence as

Nana O watched Molly's questions begin to build and brew inside of her. 'I just don't get how a locket can change a person's day so dramatically' Molly said, placing her elbows on the table.

'You need to listen more and assume less, it is not the locket that changed Jacob's day, it's what the locket helped him to remember' Nana O said before swivelling in her seat to turn the hob down as the potatoes began to boil. Molly began to twiddle her fingers. 'Go on' Nana O encouraged.

'I just can't see what the locket helped him to remember that's all' she mumbled quietly, feeling embarrassed. 'The answer lies in the locket' Nana O said, becoming serious. 'Since the last time you saw me, has anything different happened or has anything begun to change?' 'Well, I guess the whole school closing thing and wishing not to be seen when I was in bed, as well as coming to see you. Ok, maybe there have been a lot of different things happening but I don't see how that has anything to do with the story' Molly said, becoming frustrated.

'Look back over that day and instead of seeing what was different did anything feel different?' Nana O prompted. 'Umm, I guess I felt safe when I was staring up at the stars like I had stepped into another world. I felt so much love from Dillon and Layla for listening to me and when I had that day dream I felt a funny feeling in my gut like it was...'. Molly stopped as the whole day began to look so different in a way she had never seen before.

Nana O leant forward on the table as she watched Molly rub her head as she tried to understand it all. Nana O got up from the table to empty the water from the pan and mash the potatoes whilst the stew warmed up. Molly decided to distract herself from her thoughts as she started to set the table. 'That's what most people do when they discover a new truth' Nana O said with her back to Molly.

Molly stopped what she was doing. 'What do you mean? We need to set the table as dinner is nearly ready' she proclaimed. 'People do that too' Nana O chuckled. Molly slammed down the mats and sat back down. 'Fine. I won't lay the table' she announced, crossing her arms across her chest. Nana O brought across Molly's dinner plate, placed it in front of her and slid a knife and fork next to it. She then went to fetch her own plate. Molly thought through gritted teeth 'I was only trying to help'. 'I'm not mad at you for setting the table. You're right, it did need setting. It was more about the true reason behind why you were setting it in the first place' Nana O said, just before she took a large forkful of potato.

'And how do you do that?' Molly asked, picking up her fork as her stomach rumbled at the smell of food. Nana O smiled as she took another mouthful of potato and raised her eyebrows in response. Molly let out a moan and began to eat. Sometimes it was like deciphering cryptic code with her Nana O.

'You have the answer. You just think it's too strange or too different to believe that it could possibly be the truth' Nana O said. Molly looked up at her and went back to eating her dinner. Maybe it wasn't such a good idea staying over; she was becoming more agitated by her Nana O's little games.

They continued to eat their dinner in silence. Molly looked up at her Nana from time to time. She always looked so peaceful like all she had to think about was today. When they had both finished, Molly moved across and took the plates. Taking them to the sink, she began to wash up the pots.

Nana O got up and put the kettle on for another cup of tea. They then both made their way back into the living room. Molly headed towards the fire and put another log on; the fire roared from its embers into life.

Molly walked across to the sofa, picked up the blanket and wrapped it around herself again. Nana O took her usual spot in her chair. 'Could you explain it to me with a little less cryptic code and a little more simplicity?' Molly asked sympathetically. 'Now, where would the fun be in that?' Nana O chuckled to herself. 'Please, Nana, I want to understand' Molly pleaded.

'Very well, you know how I said that the story was about one of the universal laws, that we are all one, well this means that we are all connected in some way. There is a part inside all of us that is the same. You came across that part when you had the dream about the storm. There are many names for this part, but today we will call it our intuition'.

'But what you need to understand is that this part of us cannot be seen, only felt, and most of the time it may only be one person's intuition that is triggered. The more you listen the more it occurs. However, the key lies in the locket's answer. You can only feel your intuition clearly when you are in a state of love. That's why, when Jacob found things that he loved, his life became better, because he was able to listen to his internal guidance guiding him, giving him direction, protecting him as he began to follow it more!'

Molly nodded. 'Then what was that all about at the kitchen table?' Molly asked. 'When we find a truth it may make people feel a little uncomfortable. They either distract themselves or go into denial, trying to lie that it never happened in the first place. Some people become curious about what it is, like you have become' Nana O replied softly.

'It's ok to know about it but we have been given it for a reason and it starts with understanding that reason' she continued. 'Life is not meant to be about resistance and fighting our way through, simply surviving. It is meant to be a chance to remember, to learn, to love. Now this doesn't mean that it will be easy but it's our choice whether or not we have fun along the way. The challenges are there to show you that there is a part of you that you have forgotten, and it is giving you an opportunity for you to remember'.

'But most of us have forgotten about those parts of ourselves for a reason and that reason is normally because of an experience we had where we got scared, or it was too painful, there are many reasons. But just like a broken mirror, you only see fragments of the picture being reflected. The experiences help you to remember and return the pieces of yourself that have been lost and eventually you become whole once more' Nana O said with enthusiasm.

Molly slid down the sofa, resting her head on the sofa arm as the warmth of the fire and her Nana O's soothing voice floated around her. She finally became relaxed, not from being away from the anger but relaxed with the whole of life.

'A lot of the time, people ignore their intuition because it may not seem logical to them. But most of all it is because it incurs change and sometimes it is not always easy to move through the illusion of the pain to reach and recover the part that had been hiding for so long. Like I said, it can be fun if you wish it to be' Nana O said, motioning across to where Molly was now lying on the sofa.

'Why don't they want it to be fun?' Molly inquired. 'Ah, because they believe that the only way they deserve something is through struggle. They do not notice the gift that they receive every day because it isn't some grand gesture like winning money or a holiday of a lifetime. The gift may simply be a rose, a smile or a moment getting lost in laughter'.

'The locket helped Jacob to remember something that he thought had gone, that was only hiding beneath the fear of a memory. When he found the locket he found a piece of himself, love, and when that returned, his life transformed. As he discovered a part of himself so he discovered a new part of life'. Nana O looked in front of her as Molly's eyes began to droop with tiredness. She stayed silent as Molly's eyes fell shut. Nana O got up and placed the blanket so it covered Molly's body and put another log on the fire.

She returned back to her chair to look out the window to see the owl sitting in the tree opposite her cottage. The room began to get warm as the fire burned bright. Nana O closed her eyes and slept with a smile on her face.

6 TRIALS AND TEARS

Molly woke the next morning to the sound of clanking pots and pans from the kitchen. She opened her eyes, looked across to the empty chair opposite her and reached up, bringing her arms above her head and stretched, feeling her body begin to come alive from its slumber.

Molly threw back the blanket and swung her feet to the floor, pausing a moment to let her body readjust as she felt light headed. 'Breakfast's ready!' she heard Nana O call from the kitchen. Molly reluctantly pushed herself off the sofa and shuffled across the living room the way Nana O did. With every step she felt her legs begin to wake up and function again.

Molly appeared at the kitchen doorway. Nana O was already sitting at the kitchen table taking a bite out of a bacon sandwich. Molly took a deep breath in 'That smells so good' she said as her stomach rumbled in agreement. Nana O motioned for Molly to join her at the kitchen table where there was another bacon sandwich waiting.

'How did you sleep?' Nana O asked as she swallowed her mouthful. 'Incredibly well' Molly said as she rubbed the sleep out of her eyes, 'And actually no bad dreams which is strange'. 'Strange? Maybe the answers you were seeking through your dreams have been found so your mind can now rest' Nana O replied, dusting the crumbs off her chest.

'Do you mean what we were talking about last night?' Molly asked before taking another bite out of her bacon sandwich. 'Possibly' Nana O replied, 'Does this mean that I can have an incredible day, just like Jacob from the story?' Molly asked wishfully. 'Every day has the potential to be extraordinary, but not all days are. As you learn to enjoy life's rhythm, the ebb and flow, some days are epic, others are disasters – all are relative' Nana O said, pushing her chair back as she stood up and made her way across to the kettle.

'The rhythm?' Molly asked, confused. 'Yes, but we'll save the story of that universal law for another day. I think you have had enough learning about oneness and following your intuition. It's all well and good knowing the theory behind it but it's not until you go out and experience it do you truly understand them' Nana O said as the kettle came to the boil and she filled the teapot with water.

'Isn't knowing and understanding the same thing?'
Molly asked, picking up her plate and taking it to the
sink. Nana O smiled and let out a chuckle 'Most
people believe so. Someone could describe the taste
of a cup of tea incredibly but it's just not the same as
taking a sip for yourself. It's good to know that you
have guidance, that you have intuition, but to follow it
and have great experiences of the oneness of
everything, being no greater or lesser, but all relative,
all the same, turns what could have been something
ordinary into extraordinary, and then to be able to
follow your guidance in all circumstances, well, life
suddenly becomes exceptional'.

'But how can I follow my intuition when I can't go
wherever I want whenever I want – mum wouldn't
allow it, school wouldn't allow it' Molly said,
becoming more frustrated. Nana O brought the
freshly made tea to the table and motioned for Molly
to sit back down.

Molly plonked herself in the chair. 'I'm trapped in the
"you must do list"' Molly said, wrapping her hands
around the warm cup of tea Nana O had just poured.
'No one is ever trapped. The only thing that can trap
them is their own thinking of being trapped. The key
is to be able to follow these universal laws whilst
navigating your way through society and current
cultural perspectives. You never know, Molly, by you
being able to do that you may do something

extraordinary. You have unlimited potential inside of you, it's your choice how you wish to use it' Nana O, looking intently at Molly.

'Oh, don't start the whole "who are you going to be when you get older" question' Molly scowled. 'I'm still learning who I want to be when I grow up' Nana O said playfully. Molly smiled as she stared down into her cup of tea. 'It's not what you want to do – that's the easy part. We make to-do lists all the time. It's how you want to do it that counts. How will you approach life experiences – with love, hate, fear, courage, inspiration? – that is the true question' Nana O continued.

Molly shuffled uncomfortably in her seat, then realised what she was doing and stopped, 'I know, I know. I'm finding it hard to receive another truth'. Nana O sat silently. They were quickly interrupted by the sound of tyres on the dirt and then a screeching noise as a car came to a halt. Molly looked pleadingly at Nana O. 'I really don't want to go to school today, I really, really don't want to go home today' Molly begged.

They heard footsteps up the path. 'Please, Nana, just one more day with you' Molly begged again. The front door opened. 'Molly, where are you?' she heard her mum call. Molly sat silently, not wanting to be found. Nana O stared across at Molly sitting hunched over. 'We are in the kitchen' Nana O replied. Molly glared at Nana O. Molly's mum appeared at the kitchen door. Molly slowly turned round 'Morning, mum' she said wirily. Molly's mum thrust her school uniform at Molly. 'Go and get ready otherwise we are going to be late. And, no, you are not ill anymore – you've had your day off' Molly's mum said sternly before Molly could get her words out.

Molly gingerly got up from the table and took the uniform, making her way up the stairs to the bathroom to get changed. 'Tea's not been long made' Nana O said. 'I'm good, thanks, we'd best be off quickly and all' Molly's mum replied, still hovering in the doorway. 'Very well' Nana O said, taking a sip from her cup.

'You know you really shouldn't be filling her head with these stupid stories of wishful thinking and hope, like life is a garden of roses' Molly's mum said. Even the thought made her blood boil. 'Well my dear, if they are stupid then there is nothing for you to worry about. Molly is a bright girl and wouldn't listen to something that's stupid' Nana O replied.

Nana O looked up at her daughter standing in front of her. If only she had the power to remove the fibres of pain and hate from her life, pick them out strand by strand. But she knew deep down inside of her that she could fix things if she wanted to but no one can heal unless they are truly willing. She sighed at how many of those continue to suffer because they are afraid and only able to see things getting worse instead of better.

Molly's footsteps down the stairs brought Nana O out of her thoughts and back into reality. Nana O got up from the table. 'I'll see you in a couple of days' Molly's mum said before disappearing out of the front door. Molly turned to Nana O and walked across to where she was standing. She wrapped her arms around her and said 'I love you Nana'. 'I love you to the stars and back' Nana O replied.

'I'm not sure when I'll be seeing you again but know that I'll never be far away. Just look to the stars and you'll feel me near' Nana O said, stroking Molly's hair. 'Be the beacon of love and light this world is ready to receive, help navigate them through to better times'. Nana O took a step back and saw the young girl in front of her, 'Remember that there is unlimited potential inside of you which means you can be and do anything you want'. Nana O stepped forward and kissed Molly on the forehead.

'Don't worry, I'll come back again with mum in a couple of days' Molly replied, wondering why her Nana was acting so weird. Nana O just smiled. 'Go on, otherwise you'll be late' she said, pointing to the door. Molly gave her one last hug and skipped out the door and down the path, feeling a lot lighter and freer than she had ever felt before.

Nana O turned to watch them leave through the kitchen window. As the car disappeared down the lane a hare ran across the field opposite the cottage. Nana O smiled 'Oh I hear you loud and clear, life' she said to herself, as she went back into the living room and took one of the books off the shelf. As she flicked through the pages she found the page entitled 'wisdom from the hare'. 'Oh how fitting' she said.

Molly turned and looked out of the car window as they drove. She watched a hare leaping across the field and stop every now and again to have a look around. Molly laid her head against the headrest, knowing she was going back to a place where she felt she didn't belong.

As they drove along the road, the car swiftly moving from side to side as it glided round the corners, Molly's thoughts drifted back to the conversation she had had with Nana O the night before. She snuggled into the seat at the thought and a new feeling of peace came over her as she stared out of the window. She listened as her mum spent the journey flicking through the radio channels.

As the school gates came into sight Molly saw Dillon and Layla standing together waiting for her arrival. She smiled as she became excited to share all that she has learnt.

'I'll see you back home after school' Molly's mum said as the car came to a halt and she turned in her seat to face Molly. Molly unclipped her seat belt and looked up at her mum. 'Thank you for letting me stay at Nana O's last night, it was, well … it was magical'. Molly's mum stared at Molly intently as she saw a look she knew well. It was a look she used to have.

Molly watched her mum's expression soften. 'Why did you stop believing in the stories?' Molly asked inquisitively. Molly's mum's gaze drifted to the floor as she thought back to all the nights she had spent by the fire. 'I never stopped believing, I just forgot and then became so distracted with life and the jobs I felt were important that I never felt I had the time to do one of the most important jobs of all, caring for myself, my happiness and thoughts' she said as she pursed her lips together with guilt.

'Maybe it is something that will come back to you in time' Molly smiled encouragingly. 'Maybe' Molly's mum said, trying to fake a smile. Molly opened the car door and slid out. Her mum sat there for a moment then saw the clock on the dashboard and quickly brought the car back to life in a hurry as she was already going to be late for work.

Molly skipped across to where Layla and Dillon were standing. 'Well, someone is feeling a lot better today' Layla said, reaching out to hug Molly. Molly gave her a squeeze back and then turned to Dillon and did the same. 'Good to have you back' he said, giving her a kiss on the cheek.

'Well I called your house last night and your mum was in such a foul mood. I asked if I could come round and see you and she bellowed down the end of the phone that you were staying at your Nana's' Layla said as she felt a shiver go down her spine. Molly chuckled 'Yeah, she wasn't too pleased with the idea. It was so strange because it's like part of her wanted me to stay and the other part of her wanted to take me away from the place where I could learn more. It was like she knew what was going to happen and she wanted to stop it from happening. It wasn't because she was trying to protect me, it was like she was trying to protect herself' Molly said. 'Well that's not nice' Dillon said as they walked across the playing field to class.

'Anyway, I have so much I have to tell you' Molly said as she bounced along. 'Ok, Skippy, calm down and start from the beginning' Dillon said as he placed his hand on her shoulder to try and keep her feet on the ground. He feared she would float off at any moment into the sky like a balloon filled with happiness.

As they walked into the school building Molly began to tell them the rest of the story and all the questions she had asked Nana O. They continued to talk as they made their way down the corridor and into the classroom. Layla and Dillon were captivated by what

Molly was saying. As Molly walked into the
classroom, placing her bag down on the desk, she said
'It's so strange. I feel lighter, freer. How can I best
describe it? Like this ghost that has been haunting me
inside has been freed, as if Nana O's words have
helped me remember something, allowing this part of
me that wasn't true to float away and leave. I don't
feel afraid to say goodbye to it, but in a strange way
I'm thankful for it for haunting me until I finally
listened, until I woke up to why it was there in the
first place'.

They all sat down in their seats as the teacher entered
the room. 'Ok Molly, this is getting a bit weird' Dillon
said, feeling uncomfortable at the thought of
someone being haunted. 'No, it's no different than
being afraid of a thought or something your
imagination has created. It's just how I like to see it.
You would probably feel better seeing it as a river
which was brown and mucky and is now flowing
crystal clear'.

'Now that I can relate to' Dillon said, beginning to
feel more comfortable again. 'I wonder what I have
inside of me?' Layla said aloud, speaking to herself.
Molly shrugged her shoulders as they heard the
teacher pretend to cough to get everyone's attention.

As they opened up their exercise books, Molly tore a
page out and wrote 'I now understand that no matter
what fears we have inside they don't have to stay

115

there forever. We can let them out, set them free'. She turned around and handed it to Layla. Layla read the note and passed it onto Dillon. As Dillon read it he felt an elbow in his side from Layla. He looked up and saw the teacher walking towards him.

Before he could hide the note the teacher's hand was in front of him and held out flat, gesturing for the note. Dillon sheepishly took the note from his lap and laid it on the teacher's hand. The teacher read what had been written and then looked at the three of them. He turned and made his way back to the front of the class, not saying a word, placing the note down on his desk. They quickly scurried to get on with the work that had been set, not saying a word to each other for the rest of the lesson.

As the school bell rang for break, the teacher called above the rustle of bags and coats 'Molly, Dillon and Layla I want you to stay behind. I need a word with you' as he picked up the note from his desk. The three of them looked at each other, fear flashing across their faces, as they sat back down in their seats. They watched the rest of their classmates filter out of the classroom and into the corridor.

The teacher's footsteps echoed around the empty classroom as he made his way up to where they sat. He perched himself on the desk opposite them, 'So are you going to tell me who wrote this note?' he inquired, waving it in the air. They looked at each other. Dillon opened his mouth to speak, only to be interrupted by Molly. 'I did, Sir'. The teacher looked at them, took the note that he was holding in his hand and placed it in front of Molly.

'Wise words, where did you get them from?' he asked. 'Umm, myself' Molly stammered with disbelief. The teacher stood up, 'Hhmm. Well just don't let me catch you passing notes around the class again' he said as he made his way across the classroom and out the door.

The three of them looked at each other. 'That was lucky' Dillon said, grabbing his stuff and making a quick exit out of the classroom with Molly and Layla following swiftly behind him. They walked down the corridor 'Maybe we should talk about this after school' Layla said, hating the thought of getting into any more trouble. 'Oh come on, Layla, live on the wild side' Dillon said, pretending to act like a tiger. Molly and Layla looked at each other, linked arms and pushed Dillon out of the way, watching him bounce off the corridor wall.

'Ok, ok, we'll talk about it later on' he said, coming up behind and slotting between the two of them, draping his arms across both of their shoulders as they walked to their next class.

Molly sat in class watching the hands on the clock move slowly around. If they went any slower we would be going back in time she thought to herself as the teacher put the next slide up on the board. Molly shuffled uncomfortably in her seat. She was beginning to get restless, wanting the day to end so that she, Dillon and Layla could go and sit on the playing field to discuss what Nana O had said.

Molly looked back up at the clock; one more minute had gone by and she let out a groan. Molly felt her bag begin to vibrate. She slipped her hand down the side of the desk to get out her phone and turned it over to see the screen. There lighting it up was a message from her dad. As she clicked on the message Molly read the words 'Come straight home after school!' Molly elbowed Layla who was sitting next to her to show her the screen. Layla screwed up her face in response. 'What's that all about?' she whispered. Molly shrugged and shoved her phone back in her bag.

Molly's mind began to race. 'What if mum and dad are going to tell me they are getting divorced? What if I have to pick who I want to live with tonight? What if something has happened to Nana O? What if she has been rushed into hospital?' Molly began to rub her hand on her forehead in an attempt to rub away her worries. She felt her hand get gently lowered back to the table. 'I don't think it's anything major. It is probably just about you sleeping over at Nana O's last night' Layla said soothingly. Molly glanced across looking more worried than ever.

Their discussion was broken up by the bell signalling it was lunchtime. Molly reached down and pulled out her phone from her bag and texted back 'What's wrong?' She sat waiting, staring at the phone to signal a response. The phone vibrated in her hand, 'We'll speak tonight!' he replied. Molly grabbed her bag and ran out of the classroom. She ran out of the school building, across the playing field and towards her favourite tree where she threw down her school bag in fury and rage, as tears streamed down her face.

Layla and Dillon were in quick pursuit and came to a standstill as they reached the tree, watching Molly pacing up and down muttering to herself. 'What's up?' Dillon asked tentatively. Molly shot round glaring at him. Dillon took a step back as he had never seen Molly like this and it scared him. 'What's up? I'll tell you what's up! The lies, the deceit, all because they don't have the bottle to say the truth, not due to politeness but because the truth scares them!'

'Why is it that we have to suffer every day and not enjoy what we could do? And most of all, why do I have to sit and listen to that twaddle?' Molly concluded, thrusting her finger towards the school. Layla and Dillon erupted into laughter. Molly began to cry more, headed towards her bag and slung it on her shoulder as the anger inside reached boiling point.

She fought the internal conflict as all the illusions
began to break away. Dillon motioned for her to stay,
trying to catch his breath from laughing so hard.
'Molly, wait' he gasped. 'We weren't laughing at you,
we were laughing at the word twaddle. Where did you
hear that?' he said, as he began to laugh again.

Molly scowled at him for not taking her seriously.
'Never mind' she said in dismay as she began to make
her way across the playing field – not towards school
but towards home. 'Wait. Where you going?' Layla
shouted as they watched Molly walk away. 'To find
the truth. I need answers' Molly replied through
gritted teeth. Layla began to follow. As she moved
she felt a hand take her arm. She turned round to see
Dillon who was holding her back 'Let her go, I think
this is something she needs to find out for herself'.

They both stood watching Molly making her way
across the grass until she disappeared behind some
trees. As she walked across the path she began to
recall all the memories she had, trying to find answers,
trying to understand what Nana O had said. She
thought about the memory about the part of us that
we all have inside that connects us. She sat down on
the edge of the kerb, staring out in front of her.

'Find something you love, to hear your guidance from
above' Molly whispered. She thought back over her
life and then looked around her and began to cry
more. 'How can I find something I love when there is

no love around me at all?' Molly sat weeping in her hands, as she listened to the footsteps of people passing her by.

Then she felt a presence. She looked up to see a woman standing next to her holding a bunch of flowers. The lady pulled a lily from the bunch and handed it to Molly. 'Have a lovely day' she said and the lady continued on her way. Molly sat in disbelief at the flower that lay in her hand. 'Why would someone do that?' she asked and then looked back to where the lady had disappeared off into a crowd.

As she moved the flower between her fingers, Molly began to feel the silk-like petals. A gentle breeze drifted the sweet scent around her nose and the pure colours glistened in the sunlight. Molly began to smile as she realised she had never truly looked at a flower before. What generosity from a person she didn't know. Molly looked up and around where she sat. Everything became more vibrant, colours appeared brighter, just like the night when Nana O began to tell the story of the locket.

Molly felt a warmth inside, as if the pieces of herself that she felt were lost were now returning and the cracks from the lies she had been told were disappearing. She looked back down at the flower and thought about how, for the first time, she felt like she was blooming too. She felt for the first time in a long time that she was whole again.

Molly looked up to notice a bus stop opposite to where she was sitting. She had been so busy being angry that she hadn't taken any notice of it. Molly rose to her feet with the flower still in her hand. As she stood there on the kerb she felt a new strength inside, not that things were going to be any easier but that she would always have the help she needed to navigate her way through the changes. 'Intuition! That's what Nana O called it' Molly yelled with excitement, as people stared at her as they passed by.

Molly skipped across to the bus stop and found the bus number that would take her to the end of Nana O's lane. Molly stood waiting, humming and waving the flower through the air with delight. When she became distracted by an oncoming car Molly squinted as she recognised it as it moved closer. As the car pulled in next to the bus stop she froze as she saw her dad in the driver's seat. The window slid down as Molly's dad leant across. 'I think you had better get in' he said sternly.

Molly let the flower flop down by her side as her arm lay limp. She opened the car door and climbed in. As Molly closed the door the car sped off from the bus stop and her dad did not say a word. They drove in silence as they made their way back to the house. Molly watched the traffic lights change from green to red and wondered if it was worth jumping out and running as fast as she could. She decided not to as she continued to stroke the petals of the flower, wishing she could be back in that happy place again.

The car turned down the road, up the drive and shunted to a stop outside the house. Molly watched her dad get out and march to the front door where he disappeared into the house. Molly quietly undid her seat belt and opened the car door, stepping out onto the driveway, slowly making her way into the house.

As Molly walked through the door she was faced with her dad standing boldly with his arms folded. 'Close the door Molly' he said coldly. Molly clutched onto the flower even tighter as she closed the front door and turned to face him. 'You can imagine my surprise when I received a phone call from school saying that you hadn't shown up for class' he began. 'And then when I went there and saw Layla and Dillon they could barely get their words out and kept changing their story of where you might be. I had a wild guess at where you might be heading' he said, towering over her. Molly stood frozen to the spot.

'Do you have anything to say about the matter?' he finished. Molly shook her head, not knowing what to say, thinking he wouldn't listen anyway. Molly's dad continued to stand there staring at her as if he was waiting for something. Molly walked around him and headed up the stairs to her room.

As she reached halfway her dad announced 'And

you're grounded for the next three months for pulling a stunt like that' and he departed into the kitchen. Molly stood for a moment on the stairs and then continued up and into her bedroom, closing the door quietly behind her and dropping her bag to the floor. Making her way over to the window she climbed onto the windowsill and sat down, with the flower intertwined in her fingers.

Molly listened to her dad downstairs talking to someone on the phone, only able to make out a couple of the words but she knew what he would be talking about. She looked outside knowing that she would probably be spending a lot of time over the next three months looking out of this window. As she sat there she thought about Nana O and how they would probably even stop her seeing her.

A single silent tear holding a thousand memories rolled down her cheek as she thought about what was to come. She heard her dad's footsteps begin to make his way up the stairs and she quickly wiped away the tear. She turned to look out of the window again when she heard her bedroom door open. 'Your mum is on her way home and then we will have that talk' he said, looking at Molly sitting there. Molly said nothing and continued to look out of the window. Molly's dad shook his head – he hated seeing her like this. He stepped back and closed the door, making his way back down the stairs into the kitchen.

7 LOVE TRANSFORMED

Molly listened as she heard her mum's car pull into the driveway, and the car door close shut. Molly's dad made his way down the hallway just as Molly's mum opened the front door. Molly's mum stopped in her tracks, shocked to see Molly's dad standing there. 'Where is she?' Molly's mum said quietly. Molly's dad nodded up the stairs. Molly's mum nodded in acknowledgement and made her way down the hallway into the kitchen.

Molly listened from upstairs and heard the whispers but she was not able to make out what they were saying. Then she heard her dad 'Molly could you come downstairs into the kitchen please?' he called from the bottom of the stairs. Molly turned and scowled at the door. 'Why was he being nice all of a sudden?' Molly thought suspiciously as she climbed down off the windowsill.

As she passed her bed she picked up the blanket she had taken to Nana O's. Her mum must have brought it in from the car earlier that morning. Wrapping it around her shoulders again she opened the bedroom door and made her way down the stairs. As she reached the bottom, Molly stared at the front door. Something was different, something felt off, maybe even odd.

She swung herself around the banister and walked towards the kitchen. As she entered the kitchen Molly saw her dad leaning against the worktop with a cup of tea in his hand and her mum sitting at the kitchen table with her hands also wrapped around a cup of tea. They both looked at each other as Molly entered the kitchen.

Molly moved across and joined her mum at the table, taking a seat that was also facing her dad. She sat there quietly, waiting for the lecture on running away in school time to begin. A few moments passed by and no one said anything. Molly began to get even more nervous as she knew that this meant she was in a serious amount of trouble.

Molly's dad was the first to speak. 'Molly, we have some bad news to tell you' he said. Molly's face turned to shock, not because of the bad news but because it wasn't about her skipping school. Molly's mum continued to stare into her tea. 'It's about Nana O' he continued. Molly leapt to her feet. 'What's wrong? What's happened? Where is she?' Molly gasped.

'Sit back down' Molly's mum said, starting to become aware of what was happening around her. Molly slowly lowered herself back into her seat. 'This morning after I had dropped you off at school, I was at work when I received a phone call from the hospital explaining that Nana O had been taken into hospital and was on a ward. I went straight there but when I reached the hospital Nana O had already gone back to the stars' Molly's mum said faintly.

Molly stared at the table and tried to process what she was hearing, listening to her mum's words becoming broken between the tears that she was trying to hold back. Molly looked up. 'What time was this?' she asked. She watched the disbelief on their faces in the way she was reacting. 'About 12:30 I guess, not long before I had found you at the bus stop' Molly's dad replied, confused.

Molly looked out in front of her as she continued to process everything that had happened earlier that day. Molly stared at her dad and, not saying a word, she suddenly sprang from her seat and disappeared upstairs. 'Molly, what is it?' Molly's mum called in disbelief. They listened as they heard the thump of Molly's feet as she came back down the stairs, re-appearing in the kitchen.

Molly made her way back to the table, pulling the blanket back around her as it had fallen off when she had leapt from her seat. When she was settled again,

Molly lifted the flower from her lap that she had received earlier on that day. Molly's mum squinted at the flower then her eyes opened wide. 'Where did you get the lily from?' she asked, not taking her eyes off the flower.

'Well, you see, something really weird happened to me just before I went to the bus stop' Molly said eagerly. Molly's mum looked at Molly's dad who just raised his eyebrows in response. Molly proceeded to tell them both of why she had left school earlier that morning. She told them about sitting down on the kerb and receiving the flower from the stranger who told her to have a lovely day.

Molly took a big gasp of air in as she had not taken a breath as the words poured out of her mouth. Molly's mum began to rub her forehead and then broke out into a smile. 'I'd best put the kettle back on' Molly's dad said, making his way over to the sink. 'What? I don't get it!' Molly said confused, 'What am I missing?' she asked her mum.

Molly's mum reached across and passed Molly's dad her empty cup for a refill, and then turned back to look at Molly. 'Well it wouldn't be your Nana O if she hadn't gone with some kind of flair' she chuckled. Molly sat staring at her mum none the wiser. Molly's mum recognised that look and began to explain. 'The lily flower was your Nana O's favourite flower' she said, shaking her head, still not quite believing the coincidence herself.

'And whenever she left somewhere she would always wish the person a lovely day because she believed love could never be lost, it could only transform. This meant that any moment in a day could transform into a lovely one, no matter what had happened previously' Molly's mum finished, as a fresh cup of tea was placed in front of her.

Molly sat there in awe, holding the flower up in front of her. 'Maybe that was her next lesson for you' Molly's mum said graciously. 'But how did she know? And how did she organise that the lady would find me and hand me the lily?' Molly asked, now frowning at how crazy all this seemed but having lived it herself she knew that it had definitely happened.

'Your Nana O understood some things about life that most of us try not to remember, scared of what we might find out I guess' Molly's dad stepped in, trying the best way he could to make sense of something that was beyond logic. 'I'm sure by now she will have told you the story about the man finding the locket. Well there is more truth in that story than most of us accept. If your Nana O was here she would be telling you that you were just having an experience of one of life's truths' he continued as he joined them both at the table.

'But I thought you hated Nana O telling me those stories?' Molly said, looking from her mum to her dad and back again. Molly's dad looked down into his tea as he spoke 'We didn't hate her telling you those stories. We found it hard to see you so optimistic about life. We love you dearly but you reminded us how much we had forgotten, how much we live each of our days acting like the walking dead' he said, looking up at Molly's mum.

Silence descended. 'Well maybe not all has been lost. If love can transform then maybe wisdom can too. We could always learn this stuff together' Molly said quietly as she swung her legs under the table, not quite knowing the reaction she would get.

'I think that would be a great idea' Molly's mum said, reaching across and taking hold of Molly's hand. 'We are just people too' she continued 'and even grown-ups make mistakes. I am sorry how we have handled it so far but let this be the start of a new chapter' Molly's mum said as a tear rolled down her cheek.

'I'd like that' Molly said, sliding off her chair and walking across to her mum, as she flung her arms around her neck and gave her a kiss. 'Do we have any pictures of Nana O?' Molly asked, still hugging her mum. 'Yes I believe so, on top of the wardrobe. There are some photo albums and I am sure in one of them is the photo album of Nana O. Why do you ask?' Molly's mum said, intrigued. 'Well I thought it might be a good idea for us to all start on the same page' Molly said, wiggling from side to side.

In the background they heard the doorbell ring. 'I'll get it' Molly's dad said, rising to his feet and making his way down the hallway to the front door. Molly listened to hear the person's voice. Maybe it was Layla and Dillon? She listened as she heard the door open and heard instead an older male voice. Molly let out a sigh of disappointment. She continued to listen as she heard her dad close the front door.

Molly's dad reappeared at the door holding a parcel. He reached across and handed it to Molly. 'It's addressed to you' he said, curious about what was inside. 'For me? That's weird. I haven't asked for anything'. Molly took the parcel, placed it on the table and ripped off the cardboard to uncover a scrapbook. As Molly opened up the scrapbook there was some writing on the first page.

Molly began to read it aloud. 'Life only has one answer. Yes, this means that whatever you are asking life, it says yes to it. If you are saying you haven't got something then life is saying yes you have, if you say it's on the way or you are going to have it, life says yes you are. If things don't seem to be working out then the key is to change the question. But most of all, if you don't reach your dreams or life moves in different directions don't worry, the most important thing is not to give up on yourself. Have a lovely day' signed Nana O.

Molly began to laugh and each laugh caused her to laugh even more. Her mum and dad looked at each other, smiling. 'What's so funny?' Molly's dad asked. Molly tried to form a sentence but ended up throwing her head back as the room echoed with her laughter. As the laughs began to fade, Molly looked at them both. 'I was just thinking that we should create a memory book of all the things we have learnt from Nana O and life. We can keep adding to it as we go. As I was thinking about this, like magic, this one arrives' Molly said as she flicked through the blank pages.

'It looks like Nana O had the same idea' Molly's mum said as she ran her fingers over the cover of the book. 'I'll go and fetch the photographs' she said as she got up from the table and made her way upstairs. 'I'll go and get my coloured pens' Molly said, racing down the hallway and up the stairs to her school bag. She pulled out her pencil case and ran back into the kitchen, sliding along in her socks on the tiled floor, crashing into the kitchen table.

Molly's mum reappeared in the doorway holding a photo album. Molly's mum and dad gathered either side of Molly who was sitting in the middle. Molly reached across the table and pulled the scrapbook closer and then took the photo album that her mum was still holding and placed it in front of her.

As she turned the first page there was a picture of Nana O outside her cottage. Molly felt a wave of sadness wash over her and sink deep into her heart. 'I don't like the idea that she is not there anymore and that I will never see her again' Molly muttered, as tears began to well up. Molly's dad put his arm around her and kissed her on the top of her head.

'Like she said, love is not lost but only transformed, and even though she is not physically around anymore, as we have experienced today, she is still very much a part of our lives' he said gently. 'I guess' Molly replied, wiping away her tears.

Molly continued onto the next page and there laid a collage of photographs of Nana O with different people, some in exotic countries. 'Nana O sure did like to travel' Molly said, amazed. 'She used to say that when her body could no longer handle the journeys, she would continue the journeys through her imagination, to new places' Molly mum said as she smiled.

Molly turned to the next page and there lying in the centre of the page was a picture of Nana O holding a lily next to her heart. 'I think we should use this one' Molly said as she began to take it out of the photo album. She turned it over, smeared the back of the picture with glue and placed it on the front of the scrapbook.

'I agree that thàt is the perfect choice' Molly's mum said as she admired the photograph. Molly opened up the scrapbook to the first page where Nana O had left her a message. She took the photo of Nana O in front of her cottage from the photo album and stuck it at the bottom of the message. Molly looked at the page. 'Do you think I'll ever be that wise?' Molly asked. 'I think you already are' Molly's dad replied as he admired the miracle sitting next to him.

Molly turned to the next page in the scrapbook which was blank. 'I guess it's our turn to add to it' Molly's dad said, taking his arm away from around Molly. 'I think I have one to start us off with' Molly's mum said. As she flicked through the photo album she stopped at a photo of Nana O in her younger years. She was on a swing with her legs up in the air. She took out the photograph and placed it in the scrapbook. Taking a purple pen from Molly's pencil case she wrote 'The more you let go of worry and "what ifs", the more room you have for love and "what is"'.

She placed the pen back on the table. 'This is definitely something I need to do more of' she said as she looked at Molly's dad. 'You and me both' he said as he stroked her hair. Molly began to flick through the photo album and stumbled across a picture of

Nana O standing drenched on top of a big hill in the countryside.

She peeled out the photograph and stuck it in the centre of the page of the scrapbook. She reached out to take a green pen and began to write, 'Don't fear the challenge, welcome the opportunity'. 'I guess it's my turn to add to the scrapbook' Molly's dad said as he turned to the next blank page. He picked up the photo album and brought it closer to him.

He closed it up and whispered to the book 'Take me to the picture for me'. The book parted slightly in his hands. He proceeded to open the book up at that page and there was a picture of a close up of Nana O's face as she smiled a mischievous smile with a twinkle in her eye. Molly turned to her dad 'What was that all about?' she said, flabbergasted. 'You're not the only one who knows a trick or two' he said as he took the picture out and transferred it to the scrapbook.

As he took a red pen, he began writing above the picture. 'Nana O sat me down one night in front of the fire and told me these words: "There is something inside all of us that is untouchable and unbreakable. It's this part that carries us through our challenges, giving us strength when we feel we can't, showing us that we can"' Molly's mum began to giggle. 'I remember that night. You walked out that cottage so confused saying Nana O had finally lost all her marbles'. Molly's dad began to giggle too. 'Yeah, I remember. Then the very next day that was exactly what I needed to know when I got fired from that job and then by the afternoon I had found this one'. He began to shake his head, saying 'She definitely did have brilliant timing'.

Molly turned back to the photograph book but this time she closed it like her dad had and whispered to the book: 'Show me the photograph which matches this thought'. The book parted slightly. Molly opened it up and there was a photograph of Nana O standing in front of a sunset, holding out her hands to the side of her as the sun was setting. It surrounded Nana O's body in red, purple and yellow, and her hands were outlined by the light.

Molly took the photograph and put it in the scrapbook. She took an orange pen and wrote these words around the picture: 'Just because the rest of us can't see it, doesn't mean it's not real. Just because it hasn't been done before doesn't mean it can't come true'. Molly smiled knowing that whatever lay ahead she would make it through.

Molly's mum took the photograph album again and flicked through. She found a photograph of Nana O in her favourite chair by the log fire. She took it out, 'I know exactly what piece of wisdom is meant to go with this photograph' Molly's mum said as she took it out and stuck it in the scrapbook. She picked up a pen and wrote 'I know more about life today than I knew yesterday, but not as much as I will know tomorrow'.

Molly closed the scrapbook and smiled at the photograph on the front. 'I guess this is what she means by love transformed. It kind of feels like she is here with us whilst we remember some of life's truths' Molly's mum said. Molly's dad wrapped his arms around Molly's mum, sandwiching Molly in between them. 'I probably don't say this enough but I love you both to the stars and back' he said.

Molly's mum and dad got up from the table and made their way across the kitchen as they began to get the ingredients out for dinner. In the background they heard the chime of the phone ring in the hallway. Molly slid off her seat. 'I'll get it. It's probably Layla' she said as she shuffled across the kitchen. As she entered the hallway she reached and grabbed the phone. 'Hello' she said. 'Hey, it's just me' a voice replied on the other end.

'Hello just you' Molly said, chuckling. 'No, silly, it's me' Layla's voice said eagerly. 'I know it's just you' Molly said in fits of laughter. The laughter became infectious as Layla began to laugh too. Layla was the first to speak as they composed themselves. 'Well that answers that question' she said, happy to hear Molly sounding cheerful. 'What do you mean?' Molly asked, confused. 'Well, after your disappearing act earlier on today, I just had a really horrible feeling all day that something bad had happened'. There was silence on the other end of the phone. 'I guess by the silence, my intuition was right?' Layla said cautiously. Molly just stood staring at the kitchen door, wondering how she was going to tell Layla. 'Yes, your intuition was right. Hang on a second'. Molly took the phone away from her ear and placed it on her chest.

'Mum!' she yelled. 'Can Layla and Dillon come over for tea?' she continued. 'Yes, we're doing spag bol for dinner'. Molly lifted the phone off her chest and back to her ear. 'Layla, are you still there?'. 'Yep, still here and I'll be over in 10 minutes. I have already texted Dillon. He is on his way, one mention of food and he already had his shoes on'. They both began to chuckle again. 'See you in a few minutes and I'll explain everything then' Molly said as she hung up the phone and made her way back to the kitchen.

As she climbed back onto her seat she picked the blanket up off the floor. 'You know there is quite a story about that blanket' Molly's dad said, trying not to cry from chopping the onions. Molly looked down at the blanket that was now covering her body, at the individual stitches, colours and patterns. 'All I know is that it is just a blanket that Nana O gave to me when I was born' Molly replied, as she stared at her dad intently for more information.

'Yes, that is correct' Molly's mum replied, as she poured the pasta into the saucepan, wiped her hands on the tea towel and walked across to sit back at the table. 'That blanket was picked up on Nana O's very first walk about. I can't remember where, but from then onwards wherever she went, so did the blanket. When she handed it over to you she said that many hours of happiness had been spent with this blanket. Many new places had been seen and obstacles had been overcome. Many words of wisdom had been absorbed into the fibres of the blanket as each stitch was bound together with unconditional love. She hoped the blanket would protect and comfort you when you grew older and when she was no longer around. But, most of all, she wanted it to be a reminder to you to not let other people's reactions distract you from your dreams and to always follow your heart'.

Molly ran her fingers over the blanket, imagining what stories this blanket would tell if it could, what words it would say to her. She smiled as she pulled the blanket tight around her, feeling like she had a bubble of love protecting her. Molly's mum watched Molly digest the words and then, with a smile, got up and returned back to the cooking.

Molly reached across for the photo album and carried on flicking through them, looking at the many different experiences Nana O had captured with a picture. As she turned the last page of the book there at the very end was a photograph of Nana O sitting on the blanket with mountains behind her and in deep conversation with someone.

Molly took out the photograph and lifted it up, 'I wonder what they were saying to each other?' She felt a shiver go up her body. As she turned it over to put some glue on the back, there was a message in Nana O's handwriting: 'If you haven't heard it today – that thing you always wanted to be, do and have – the answer is yes you can'. Molly began to play with the edge of the blanket in shock at what had just happened.

Molly's dad was leaning against the kitchen worktop staring at Molly's shocked look. He nudged Molly's mum in the side. She looked round to see what was happening as he pointed towards Molly sitting at the table staring at the photograph in her hand. They both raised their eyebrows. 'So, are you going to let the rest of us in on the little miracle that has just happened?' he said, folding his arms across his chest.

Molly suddenly snapped out of her thoughts and looked across to her dad. 'Well, I was just thinking about the blanket and if it could talk what it would say, and then I found this photograph of Nana O sitting on the blanket talking to someone with lots of wrinkles' Molly said, staring at the photograph a little closer. 'And then when I went to stick it in the scrapbook it already had the words written on it in Nana O's writing' Molly said in disbelief.

Molly's dad uncrossed his arms, 'What a coincidence. Well, what did it say?' he asked inquisitively. 'If you haven't heard it today – that thing you always wanted to be, do and have – the answer is yes you can' Molly repeated. Molly's dad stared out in front of him as he thought about the words. He took a deep breath in and let out a sigh. Molly's mum stopped stirring the sauce and stared at her husband. She had never seen him look so peaceful before.

'They are definitely some wise words to live by' he began, and broke out into a beaming smile. 'It still amazes me' he said, shaking his head and trying to shuffle his thoughts around to form some sort of sentence. 'It's all connected' he said, turning and looking at Molly's mum. 'I mean, all of it. I think I have just got it. It doesn't just mean that just us humans are one. It means life is one, us, the animals, the people we meet, what we are thinking at a given moment, how we are feeling, what we experience, what we receive, it's all the same, every aspect of life. It just looks different and takes different forms'.

He frowned as he couldn't quite believe the words he was saying. Molly shuffled in her seat, sitting up taller. She placed her hands clasped together on the table and looked firmly at her parents. 'Of course it is, we are all one, we are made out of the same basic ingredients and we just choose which experience makes our future choices. But if we really listen then we can always go back to the very core of ourselves and find our true direction because we all have intuition. If you think about it, this means "inner tuition", which helps us learn from our experiences and remember who we are, giving us guidance from the place that we originated from' Molly announced.

The room was filled with silence as all three of them stood, not quite knowing how to react to the words of wisdom that had just filled the room. Molly's mum was the first to speak. 'I think we have a mini Nana O' she said, winking at Molly's dad. He began to beam whilst walking across to Molly and wrapping her in his arms, giving her a big squeeze, 'My miracle, that's what you are'.

The door bell rang. 'That must be Layla and Dillon' Molly said, muffled by her dad's hug. He didn't move but just kept on hugging her. 'I'd best go and get that' Molly chuckled as she wriggled out of his arms and skipped down the hallway.

Molly opened the door to find Layla and Dillon rushing through, whipping off their shoes. 'So what's happened?' Dillon asked as he tried not to topple over whilst taking off his last shoe. Molly began to bounce up and down on the spot with excitement. 'I have got so much to tell you' she said, then hopped down the hallway back into the kitchen. Layla and Dillon followed on behind Molly who rushed to the scrapbook. She stuck in the photo of Nana O on the blanket and then took a gold pen out of her pencil case and copied what had been written on the back of the photograph onto the scrapbook page.

Layla and Dillon appeared at the kitchen door. 'Hi you two' Molly's mum said. 'Hi' they said in unison. 'It smells delicious' Dillon said, licking his lips as his stomach rumbled. 'It will be ready in a few minutes' Molly's dad replied as he took out the placemats and cutlery and began to set the table. Molly was soon joined at the table by Layla and Dillon who stared at Molly who was neatly writing in the scrapbook in front of her.

'What's that?' Layla asked, turning her head to the side so the writing was no longer upside down. 'Is this something to do with what happened today?' Dillon jumped in with the next question. Molly remained silent as she was in deep concentration, trying to write in her best handwriting.

Molly's mum and dad appeared at the table with a plate in each hand and placed them in front of Layla and Dillon. 'Thank you' they both said, no longer interested in the book but in the food in front of them. Molly's dad disappeared back into the kitchen to get his plate.

Molly closed the scrapbook and moved to the place where her plate had been put. Molly's dad joined them as they sat around the table. 'Tuck in' Molly's mum gestured to Layla and Dillon. Dillon dived in, scooping up a large amount of pasta and trying to fit it all into his mouth at once. 'Would you like a shovel with that?' Layla said, scowling at Dillon and his table manners. They all began to laugh apart from Layla who didn't see what was so funny.

'So, spill the beans. What happened that you couldn't tell us over the phone?' Layla asked, neatly twirling some pasta on her spoon in an effort to entice Dillon to do the same. Molly motioned to her mouth which was currently full of spaghetti bolognaise, as she chewed quickly and swallowed her mouthful.

'Well, you know after I had left you guys at school...' Molly started. 'Don't you mean flat out ran from us at school?' Dillon said with a mouthful of food. He received another scowl from Layla. Molly smiled 'Ok, maybe that too. A string of really weird things happened. Actually, come to think of it, today has been freakily weird, but in a good way'.

Molly put down her knife and fork and began to tell Layla and Dillon of all the events that had happened that day … from the flower, to Nana O dying, and then about the scrapbook. Everyone remained eating quietly, listening intently to what Molly was saying, trying to keep up as she spoke faster and faster, becoming more excited.

When she reached the end of the day, everyone had

eaten all their food and no one spoke. Molly glanced round, looking at the different expressions on the faces in front of her. She picked up her knife and fork and continued to eat her dinner. 'That's so unbelievable, brilliant!!!' Dillon pronounced, flailing his arms up in the air. 'Seriously, that's so incredible!!! Not the bit about Nana O dying but the rest is utter genius. How did she do it?!' he said, leaning back in his chair in admiration. The whole room proceeded to erupt into laughter at Dillion's outburst.

8 LOOKING TO THE STARS

As Molly began to clear the table of the dinner plates, Layla and Dillon continued to talk with Molly's parents as a fountain of questions emerged after hearing about the events of the day. Molly meandered to the kitchen in a daze, still not quite believing that today had really happened. As she put the plates in the sink she thought that this was maybe all a dream and that she was going to wake up at any minute or that her imagination had just had a field day.

Molly let out a large yawn as she made her way back to the table, plonking herself down in her seat. She rested her elbows on the table and cupped her head in her hands. The day had finally caught up with her as her body became heavy and tiredness set in. 'Well, we have all had quite a day and I think it's time to call it a day' Molly's mum announced as she glanced at Molly's eyes that were barely staying open.

Dillon let out a groan. 'I guess' he said unenthusiastically, not wanting to leave. Layla popped up out of her chair. 'Thank you for dinner' she said as she pushed her chair under the table. Dillon slowly rose, hoping that they would change their mind and all sit back down again. He felt an arm link with his and haul him up. 'Thank you' Dillon said as he was dragged by Layla to the front door.

Molly lifted up her arm and waved meekly. 'See you on Monday, Molly' Layla shouted before disappearing out of the front door, followed by Molly's mum. Molly listened to the front door click close and let out a sigh. She got up from her chair, took hold of the blanket and walked round the table to where her dad was still sitting and gave him a kiss. 'Nan night' she said. He wrapped his arms round her and gave her one of his big squeezes. 'I'm so proud of you' he whispered.

Molly's mum reappeared at the kitchen door. Molly moved across and gave her a hug and kiss. 'Nan night' she murmured. 'Nan night sweetheart' her mum said as she kissed Molly on the forehead. Molly made her way down the hallway in a daze, dragging the blanket behind her. She pulled herself up the stairs, leaving behind the light conversation she could hear her parents having in the kitchen.

As Molly reached the top of the stairs and made a beeline for her room, her bed had never looked so luscious. She walked into her room, closed the door behind her, passed her bed and switched on her bedside lamp. She stood motionless for a second, paralysed as the thought sunk a little deeper that Nana O would not be there to greet her when she got to the cottage.

A tear rolled down Molly's cheek. Even after all she had learnt today, a part of her was still sad that Nana O was physically no more. As the tears continued to roll down her cheeks she made her way to the windowsill and pulled herself up. Pulling the blanket over her legs and closing the curtains, she created a little cave. Molly stared out of the window up at the stars. She looked at the different flickering white lights dancing in the sky.

She felt a warmth inside begin to grow. She couldn't be sad and stare at the stars at the same time. She rested her head on the window pane. 'Can you just let me know you're still around Nana O wherever you are now?' she whispered. She stared intently at the stars, waiting for a shooting star or something similar to cross her path. She continued to wait and wait.

'I guess not. Maybe you really have gone forever' Molly said as the thought made her stomach churn. Molly continued to sit there, hoping that something would happen. She looked at the sky and wondered about what else was up there amongst all the stars. She heard footsteps begin to make their way up the stairs.

She opened the curtains a crack and peeped her head out in order to hear more clearly. She heard another set of footsteps coming up the stairs and thought that it must be mum and dad going to bed. Molly had one more glance out the window just in case something had happened whilst she hadn't been looking, but there was still nothing.

Molly slid off the windowsill, her feet landing on the soft bedroom carpet. She made her way across her room to the bed, leaving the curtains slightly parted so that she could still see the stars from her bed. As she reached and took hold of the corner of her duvet, there on her pillow was a single white feather.

Molly looked around the room. No one else was there and she hadn't heard her door open. Molly looked again at the feather that lay there. She slowly reached out, expecting it to just be an illusion. Molly took hold of the feather in her fingers, laying it on the palm of her hand.

Molly climbed into bed, snuggled under the duvet and held the feather out in front of her. A smile beamed across her face. 'I knew you wouldn't just leave. You're too nosey for that Nana O' Molly said, looking at the feather. Molly took the feather and placed it under her pillow. 'Nan night, Nana O' she said and switched off her bedside lamp, leaving the stars softly lighting her room.

As the morning sunshine streamed through the gap in the curtains, Molly's eyelids fluttered as she adjusted to the morning light. She pulled up her duvet that had been a warm cocoon whilst she had slept. Molly gradually opened her eyes and scanned the room. A thought then flashed through her mind and she quickly reached under her pillow and pulled out the white feather that Nana O had placed the night before.

Molly pulled herself up into a sitting position and propped herself against the headboard. She let the feather gently roll around as she passed it from one hand to the other, then there was a knock at her bedroom door. The door creaked open slowly as Molly's mum peered through the gap. As she saw that Molly was already awake she continued to push the door open and entered the room.

Molly's mum walked across and perched herself on the edge of Molly's bed, watching Molly with the white feather. 'I see you had a visitor last night' Molly's mum said, glancing across at the feather. Molly smiled and nodded her head. 'I just wanted to know if she was still around' Molly said. 'Oh, Nana O is way too nosey to not be keeping an eye on things' Molly's mum said shaking her head as she began to remember the times she had tried to have a secret but somehow Nana O always knew.

Molly chuckled to herself then looked across at her

mum, 'That's what I said too' and went back to playing with the feather. Molly's mum lifted her hand and tucked a piece of Molly's hair behind her ear. 'Sweetheart, I'm going to go up to the cottage today and you're more than welcome to join me, but I understand if it's too soon for you' Molly's mum said softly.

Molly leant her head against her mum's shoulder and stared at the floor. 'I think I would like to go with you' Molly replied. Molly's mum kissed the top of Molly's head. 'Ok, love, come down when you are ready for some breakfast and we will head over afterwards. I'll let your dad know because he was wanting to come too' Molly's mum said, kissing her again supportively.

Molly sat up. 'I thought dad hated the cottage and that's why he never went?' Molly said bewildered. 'Well, something has changed in him. I think it used to scare him a little, not that he would ever admit that but after yesterday, I think you got his curiosity stirred' Molly's mum said whilst giving a wink.

Molly's mum got up and began to make her way out of the room. When she reached the door she turned round. 'I don't suppose you would like pancakes for breakfast?' Molly's mum asked, raising her eyebrows. Molly flung back the duvet and hopped out of bed. 'I'll take that as a yes then' Molly's mum said, disappearing down the stairs.

Molly headed over to her wardrobe and rummaged through her clothes for something to wear. She threaded her legs through her trousers and pulled on a jumper then reached for her hair brush and ran it through her hair. She then ran out of her room and down the stairs, making loud thumps as she went.

Molly flew through to the kitchen, rushed to the table and jumped into the chair, taking hold of the knife and fork that were already laid out. She began to tap on the table. 'Why are we waiting?!' she began to sing. Molly's dad walked across to the table, holding a plate with the first pancake on it. 'Good morning to you too' he said, placing the plate in front of Molly and kissing her on the top of her head before heading back over to the cooker to turn over the next pancake.

Molly reached for the sugar and lemon, sprinkled them all over and then started to cut away large pieces before shoving them in her mouth. 'You have been watching Dillon's eating habits a little too closely' Molly's mum said as she came to sit at the table with her cup of tea. Molly was just about to speak with a mouthful of pancake but was stopped by the look of disapproval on her mum's face.

Molly began to chew rapidly and gulped down her pancakes. 'They are just so delicious' Molly said. 'You are definitely the best pancake maker in the world, dad!' Molly said, taking another bite. Molly's dad came across with the next pancake. 'Thank you, and for that you shall have another pancake'. Molly scooped up the last of the pancake on her plate just as her dad was placing the next pancake down. As it flopped on her plate Molly looked up with a beaming smile.

Molly's dad came and joined them both at the table. 'So, you are going to come with us to the cottage?' he said to Molly, glancing at Molly's mum's expression, judging whether it was one of approval. Molly nodded her head as her cheeks bulged with pancakes. 'We'd better get some boxes on the way' Molly's mum said, taking a sip of tea. 'And I'll bring some tools from the garage to start taking some of the shelves down' Molly's dad nodded in agreement

Molly stopped chewing and looked up. 'What's going to happen to the cottage?' Molly asked cautiously, not knowing if she really wanted to know the answer to that. Molly's dad looked straight across, signalling for Molly's mum to answer that question. 'We don't know yet, but it needs some work doing on it, fixing it up, so we will clear it out and just mend a few things and then go from there' Molly's mum replied, trying not to make the inevitable too obvious .

Molly finished the last piece of pancake and placed her knife and fork on her plate. 'So what you are really saying is that you're going to sell it?' she said, glaring at her parents for the truth. Molly's dad stepped in before an argument arose. 'Darling, we don't know what we are going to do with it but, yes, one of the options is to sell it'. 'What are the other options?' Molly asked, picking apart her dad's argument.

Molly's dad sat silent, not having an answer. 'Um, well, maybe we could have it as a holiday cottage or rent it out' he said, seeing the look of disapproval from Molly's mum. 'I like that idea. Then when you get old you can go and live there and I'll come and visit you just like mum did with Nana O' Molly said as she stood up and began to take her plate to the sink.

'Now, hang on a minute!' Molly's dad said, turning round in his chair. 'We are a few decades off that!' he exclaimed at the thought of being called old. Molly began to chuckle as she saw the playful sparkle in her dad's eye. She slowly made her way across to the hallway and watched her dad sitting poised, like a cat stalking. Molly's dad leapt out of his seat and pounced, scooping up Molly and tickling her. 'I'm not too old to tickle you though' he said as Molly howled with laughter in his arms.

Molly's mum squeezed her way past the two of them and placed her cup in the sink. 'Come on you two. Molly go and clean your teeth whilst your dad loads up the car with the tools' she exclaimed. Molly and Molly's dad moved to one side and saluted Molly's mum: 'Yes mam!' they called. 'Dismissed!' Molly's mum said, joining in.

Molly scuttled up the stairs to the bathroom whilst Molly's dad disappeared out of the front door to the garage to get his tools and load up the car.

Molly reappeared and bounced down the stairs, crashing into Molly's mum at the bottom. 'Steady on' Molly's mum said, rebalancing herself. Molly slipped on her shoes, made her way outside and jumped into the car where her dad was already sitting waiting. They both watched as Molly's mum locked the front door and made her way to the car, slipping into the passenger side.

'Don't forget, love, we need to stop off at the shop for some boxes' Molly's mum said as she clicked in her seatbelt. 'I found a bunch of boxes from when we last moved at the back of garage – that will do the job' he said, looking across at her. 'What don't you have in your garage?' Molly's mum said, shaking her head. 'Always prepared. See? You never know when you might need these things so we don't really ever need to clean out the garage' Molly's dad said in jest as he reversed off the drive. Molly's mum began to laugh 'Nice try. You're not getting out of it that easily'.

As they drove down the road, Molly rested her head on the car window and watched the world drift by.

People continued on with their day, rushing around trying to get all their jobs done or get to the next place on time. None of them realised or even cared that Nana O was no longer around.

Molly began to cry as she didn't like the thought of going to the cottage and Nana O not being there to greet her or have one of her cups of tea. Molly's dad glanced in the rear view mirror and watched the tears roll down Molly's face. 'I feel the same. It does feel weird' he said tenderly. Molly sat up in her seat, wiped her cheeks and gave a faint smile back to her dad. 'I know it all in my head that she isn't truly gone, but in my heart I still miss her being here' Molly said wearily.

'We would both join you in that boat' Molly's mum said. 'Nana O once said to me that wisdom doesn't make the journey any less bumpy, it just helps you to keep the spring in your step as you move forward and navigate your way through the changes' she added. 'I like that' Molly said, feeling some relief. 'We should add that to the scrapbook when we get back' Molly added. 'We should take a photo of us three outside the cottage today and use that' Molly's dad said, pleased with his piece of inspiration. They all nodded in agreement as they continued along the road, drawing ever closer to the cottage.

Molly's mum reached and turned on the radio and the music echoed round inside the car. Molly went back to leaning her head on the car window as they left the

buildings behind and the view was replaced with
fields and trees. Molly's dad turned down the country
road leading up to Nana O's cottage. Molly saw her
favourite tree approaching on the edge of the road
where she had previously seen the owl a few days
before. Everyone sat in silence and a knot formed in
Molly's stomach. The car slowed down to avoid a
pothole in the road. Molly looked up at the tree and
there, once again, was an owl sitting on the lowest
branch.

'Look! Look!' Molly yelled as she thrusted her finger
towards the window.
Molly's dad slammed on the brakes and the car
screeched to a halt, flinging them all forward and then
back into their seats. Molly's mum and dad swivelled
in their seats to be able to see where Molly was
pointing. As they followed the direction of her finger
they looked out of the window and saw the owl still
sitting on the branch.

'I thought owls only came out at night' Molly's dad
said with confusion. 'So did I' Molly's mum agreed.
'I'm sure this is the same owl I saw last time I was at
Nana O's' Molly said with glee. Molly's mum began to
giggle. 'Who votes that this is another one of Nana
O's tricks?' she said as her giggles grew. Molly's dad
started to move the car forward again and continue
down the road. 'It wouldn't surprise me' he said,
shaking his head. Molly enjoyed the feeling of

excitement wash over her body. It untangled the knot that she had previously had in her stomach.

Nana O's cottage came into view and Molly watched closely. 'It looks the same but feels different' Molly said, poking her head between the two front seats to get a better look. Molly's dad pulled up at the bottom of the garden near the gate, switched off the engine and the car became silent. They all sat there just staring at the cottage. None of them wanted to be the first to go in. They were still adjusting to not seeing an old lady suddenly appear at the front door.

'Well, I will say this' Molly began in a very firm tone, 'I am under no circumstances helping clear out that creepy old shed that looks like it is going to fall down at any moment'. Molly's parents' heads shot round and they began to smile. 'Really? That was the first place I was going to get you to start on' Molly's dad said jokily.

'Well, we can't sit here forever. We'd best make a start on boxing this stuff up' Molly's mum said as she opened the car door and got out. Molly's dad shook as a shiver went down his spine. Molly tapped him on his shoulder, 'Come on, stop being a pansy' she said and then leapt out of the car before he could tickle her. Molly's dad quickly followed, pretending to chase her up the garden path. They both filled the country air with laughter.

As they both ran into the house they found Molly's mum standing in the middle of the living room in front of a few boxes with writing on. Molly screeched to a halt as she looked around the room. 'What's happened?' Molly's dad asked as he made his way around the cottage. As he stuck his head through the doorways, he only found empty rooms.

Molly froze. 'Where is all Nana O's stuff?' she asked, motionless. Molly's mum couldn't get any words out between the tears; all she could do was wave a piece of paper in the air. Molly's dad returned back into the living room. As his adrenaline pumped around his body he darted to where Molly's mum was and took the piece of paper from Molly's mum's hand. Molly's mum's hand flew to her mouth as she gasped, with tears streaming down her cheeks.

Molly's dad lifted up the piece of paper and began to read aloud:

Dear my three musketeers

I hope the day finds you well. Yes, what you are seeing is correct. I took the liberty of clearing out the house as I didn't want you spending your time clearing out my life when you should be living your own.

The boxes that have been left are items that I want to give to you, things that I hope will bring you the same amount of joy and happiness as they have given me. The rest of the things I have sold or given away, you will find the money from the sales in an envelope.

I hope that you will use it to go on an adventure together, full of new experiences. You know how fond of travelling I was, well now it's your turn! Go and see the wonders of the world in nature and in people.

I have also written a few parting words to each of you. You will find the envelopes on my chair.

Until we meet again, keep trusting your intuition as it is the part that connects us all.

Nana O

They all stood frozen in silence as they thought about the words. 'She is always one blooming step ahead, always has been, always will be' Molly's dad said, not knowing whether to be angry or relieved.

Molly wiped some more tears on the sleeve of her top and made her way across to where a couple of boxes sat with her name written on them. She knelt down and opened one up. As she peered in she smiled as she saw Nana O's favourite teapot and cups.

Molly's dad made his way across to Nana O's chair and picked up the envelope with his name on it. He made his way across to the window and perched on the windowsill as he began to open it. As he sat and read, Molly's mum joined Molly, 'Look, she left me her teapot' Molly said, smiling. Molly's mum smiled back 'Good company and a good cup of tea are priceless' Molly's mum said, imitating Nana O's voice.

Molly began to giggle. Molly's mum knelt down beside Molly and opened up her box. There on top laid her green book. Molly's mum picked it up as she opened it up and flicked through the pages. Molly shuffled closer and peered at the pages. 'What is the green book about, mum?' she asked. Molly's mum smiled at the memory of the day she wrote on the first page.

'It's where I kept all the things Nana O used to say, her pearls of wisdom' Molly's mum said, looking at Molly. 'And it's the evidence that it was all true. I wasn't as open as you are when I was a little girl so Nana O brought me this book. She told me that every time I had a gut feeling about something, every time my intuition gave me guidance, to write it down. Then once it had played out, I was to write down how it had helped me' Molly's mum continued. She closed up the book and placed it back in the box.

They turned around to see Molly's dad sniffling whilst he was perched on the window, wiping away his tears. Molly's mum got up and made her way across to where he sat and put her arm around him. He looked her in the eyes, not needing to say anything but both knowing that things were going to be ok.

161

Molly watched them as she saw a side to them she had never seen before – a moment of truth and trust. Molly closed the top of her box and walked over to Nana O's chair. She picked up her envelope and sat down. Molly turned over the envelope, opened it up and took out the folded piece of paper inside. As she opened it up she began to read:

To my dearest Molly,

I could sit and write to you for hours, but I will try to keep this short and sweet. Look again in the envelope – I think you may not have seen something.

Molly opened up the envelope again and there, lying inside, was a beautiful heart-shaped locket. Molly reached inside and lifted it out of the envelope. It hung between her fingers and she watched the sunlight catch the corner of it, making it glisten. Molly gasped. 'It can't be' she said, stunned. Molly continued to read the letter.

Yes it can be! The person in the story was me. So now you know that the story is spoken with the experience of a truth that unfolded in my life. Open up the locket...

Molly laid the piece of paper down on her lap and took the locket between her fingers. She opened it up and there laid a piece of paper. Molly reached in and lifted up the piece of paper. Written on it was 'love is the answer, wishes come true, as you remember the place that connects me and you'.

Molly sat for a moment, staring at the words. 'This can't be real' she whispered to herself. She quickly placed the piece of paper in the locket, closed it up and picked up the letter to continue to read.

Yes it can be! The locket was passed down from my grandma and from her grandma before that; it is she who wrote those words. When you feel the love that is around you, that is when you are able to hear your intuition clearly. This is when you can receive the guidance from life, telling you what to do next to make your wish come true. My love has not gone, it has only transformed and it is my wish that my love can help you to hear and act on your 'inner tuition'. So, whenever you are needing help, just ask. Ask life to step in and help, then when you get that feeling inside wondering what to do next, just do it! Let the locket be your reminder.

That day you left after hearing about the locket, we saw a hare out in the field across from the cottage. Do you remember? Well, some say the hare brings great wisdom to show you that it is time to take a leap and follow your intuition.

Never think I am far away because I will always be sending my love. It will be carried by the wind. You may have started to find a white feather here and there. That's my way of showing you that my love is never far away and, just like the wind, you may not see it but if you close your eyes you can feel it whirling around you.

So never be scared to follow your guidance. It has made itself known for a reason, use it and begin to live each day with the logic of your mind but the wisdom of your heart.

I will continue to keep watching you grow from the place I now reside as I have returned to the stars once more.

Nana O

Molly rested the note on her lap and let a tear slowly seep from her eye and roll off the side of her cheek. Molly looked across to where her mum and dad were still sitting and smiled, giving them the same look of truth and trust as her dad had done earlier.

Molly's mum made her way across the room and knelt down in front of Molly. She took the locket that lay in her hands and put it around Molly's neck, kissing her on the forehead and wrapping her arms around her as she did it. Molly's dad picked up the boxes and began to take them down to the car.

Molly's mum got up and joined him as Molly continued to sit in Nana O's chair, letting her fingers play with the locket that now lay around her neck. As she let her thoughts drift, a gust of wind swept in through the front door around the living room. As it whirled around her, Molly closed her eyes and felt the love that it carried.

Molly heard the footsteps of her parents as they re-entered the living room holding hands. 'It's time to make a move' Molly's dad said, kindly. Molly nodded and got up from the chair and joined her parents. Taking her mum's hand, they looked around the empty room with only Nana O's chair left, still positioned by the fire.

They made their way out of the living room, their footsteps chiming around the empty house as they went out of the front door into the fresh air. Molly's mum closed the door behind them with one last click. 'Hang on, don't move' Molly's dad said, motioning for them to stop. He took out his camera and rested it on a nearby rock. He clicked the timer and ran back to them as the camera flashed its countdown. He snuggled in next to Molly's mum, wrapping his arm around her waist as the camera flashed.

They began to walk down the path with Molly's dad scooping up the camera as he went by. Molly walked out through the gate and climbed into the car, closely followed by Molly's mum. Molly's dad closed the gate, pausing as he took one last look at the cottage. 'Thank you' he whispered, then joined them in the car.

The car came to life as Molly's dad turned it round and began to drive back down the lane. Molly looked back through the rear window and watched the cottage getting smaller. 'Hey, look!' Molly's mum said, pointing in front of them. They all turned as they watched the owl that had been resting on the branch take flight, soaring into the sky, its white wings illuminated by the sunlight.

Molly quickly took hold of the locket as that feeling that was becoming more familiar began to rise up from inside of her heart…

Always believe.

Can You Help Us Reach 50 reviews?

We would love to hear what you thought about the book.

1. Go to Amazon

2. Type 'Naomi Sharp' into the search box and press enter

3. Click on the book

4. Scroll down until you reach the star chart

5. Click the button and write a review

Every review received is a wonderful gift each day, thank you

With gratitude,

Naomi

9 ABOUT THE AUTHOR

www.naomisharpauthor.com

Naomi began making notes when she was 10 years old, always having a notebook ready to jot down the next profound thought or idea.

Naomi began to each day write things down in her notebook. But it wasn't until 6 years on that Naomi would write her first book Living Life With The Glass Half Full, where she would be able to share her story of changing life's adversity into lessons learnt. No sooner had she finished that book she was onto her next, as she became inspired to write A Diary Of Dreams, her first fiction. Naomi describes the experience as 'downloading a story, like a movie was playing in front of me and I was writing down what was happening moment by moment'.

Naomi continues to write as her passion grows to inspire people to heal and find happiness and hope in their life. She feels storytelling is an incredible way to pass on wisdom and life's truths.

Naomi Sharp trained as an Occupational Therapist but became fascinated in how horses help people to heal not only physically but also mentally and emotionally. Her passion for understanding how we can help our bodies to heal and our dreams to become reality has brought some breath-taking experiences into her life, as well as the opportunity to meet some incredible people and places.

During the day Naomi also runs her therapy centre for individuals with a mental, physical or emotional disability to come and spend time with horses and celebrate what makes them unique.

10 OTHER BOOKS BY NAOMI SHARP

A Diary Of Dreams

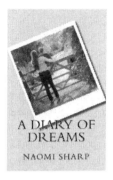

Finding love and happiness by living your dreams following the death of a family member. Hugh watched his mom Ally's happiness dissolve away as her depression took hold as all she could see was a new absence in her life of a love that was no longer there. Hugh dreamt of his mom finding her happiness, falling in love and rediscovering the magic of life, and allowing love that once was to transform as they embark on a new chapter in life. Hugh decided to create a map of dreams as a vision board of all the thing he wanted to happen in his life. This resulted in an adventure that took him and Ally to meet the people they needed to meet, the places they needed to go and the dreams they desired to experience on the road to discovering how truly magical life is. This book helps inspire you to plan and dream the life you're desiring, empowering women and children to have the courage to follow their heart's desires, and enabling their ambitions in life to flourish. An incredible story of how family, dreams and love can help you achieve anything you want.

Living Life With The Glass half Full

An inspiring true story of how a young girl chooses to learn from life's adversity with the help of horses. She travels to Ireland, France and America to understand how to live a better, happier life, and to understand what it truly means to heal. The story follows her from her younger days causing mischief in nursery through to the frustration of being dyslexic in school. This leads up to her whole world being turned around with a profound realisation. All the while different horses are guiding her path through the years with their constant friendship and companionship, highlighting some of the facts of life Naomi has picked up along the way. The book includes a bonus feature for your own personal development providing ways for you to analyse your life's problems and turn them into positives with surprising ease. It encourages you to work through your own challenges by changing your perceptions on how you view life and adversity so that you are able to change your life. This book provides a true account of how, by changing your own perceptions of life and looking for the lessons to be learnt in the adversity, the adventure of life becomes more about using those lessons to help your dreams to become your reality rather than allowing the adversity to become your future.

40 Days Transforming Your Life

 Are you ready for the journey of a lifetime, have you received enough of life's adversity that you are feeling your back is up against the wall?

Help has arrived!

In this how to book you will discover a *40 day process* that will help you and your life to transform, from a place of despair to the place where dreams come true.

You won't be doing this journey alone, every day you have a short chapter looking at what the day ahead has in store as you move up and down the emotional scale. In this 'how to' book it will explore what it means to change from the inside out and pearls of wisdom to keep you inspired and motivated to continue to move forward.

Aspects included in 40 Days Transforming Your Life

~ Letting go of past experiences
~ Loving yourself and your strengths
~ Learning to set a goal or dream
~ Setting up your routine for success
~ Celebrating your achievements
~ Worry no longer being a part of your day

40 Days Transforming Your Life book by Naomi Sharp helps you develop a simple but sustainable routine to reaching your goals, transforming your life, and living your dreams.